TABLE II. referred to in *A View of the Hard-Labour Bill,*

I. No. of Districts	II. Districts in each Circuit.	III. Place of Meeting in each District.	IV. Counties in each District.	V. Justices for each County.	VI. Convicts in a Year in each County.	VII. Convicts to be provided for in each District.	VIII. Sums to be allotted to each County. [i]
I.	*HOME CIRCUIT.* 1ft.	Chelmsford	Essex Hertfordshire	3 3	18 12	} 90 {	
II.	2d.	Maidstone	Kent Canterbury Suffex	3 1 3	26 1 6	} 99 {	
III.	3d.	Kingston	Surry	5	42	126	
IV.	*MIDLAND CIRCUIT.* 1ft.	Lincoln	Derbyshire Lincolnshire Lincoln Nottinghamshire Nottingham Rutlandshire	2 [a] 3 1 2 1 1	8 10 1 6 3 2	} 90 {	
V.	2d.	Warwick	Leicestershire Leicester Northamptonshire Warwickshire Coventry	2 1 2 2 1	4 2 7 18 5	} 108 {	
VI.	*NORFOLK CIRCUIT.* 1ft.	Bedford	Bedfordshire Buckinghamshire Cambridgeshire Ely Huntingdonshire	2 2 2 1 2	7 9 4 2 3	} 75 {	
VII.	2d.	Norwich	Norfolk Norwich Suffolk	3 1 3	15 2 14	} 93 {	
VIII.	*NORTHERN CIRCUIT.* 1ft.	Durham	Cumberland Durham Northumberland Berwick Newcastle Westmoreland	2 2 2 [b] 1 1	5 6 [c] 5 [d] 1	} [e] 51 {	
IX.	2d.	Lancaster	Lancashire	5	26	78	
X.	3d.	York	Yorkshire York Kingston	[f] 6 1 1	30 3 2	} 105 {	

[a] viz. for each of its *Parts,* one.

[b] The Town of *Berwick* is specified in §. 5. p. 7. of the Bill, among the jurisdictions comprised within the Northern circuit: but no Committee-Justices are allowed to it in §. 6.

[c] The average number of convicts for *Berwick* is computed in the lump with the number for *Northumberland.*

[d] No number of convicts is stated for *Newcastle* in the Bill: in the Table annex'd to the Bill it is stated at *five.* This makes a difference of *fifteen* in the number to be provided for.

Sections 3. 5. 6. 9. and 11.

I. No. of Districts.	II. Districts in each Circuit.	III. Place of Meeting in each District.	IV. Counties in each District.	V. Justices for each County.	VI. Convicts in a Year in each County.	VII. Convicts to be provided for in each District.	VIII. Sums to be allotted to each County. [i]
XI.	OXFORD CIRCUIT. 1st.	Oxford	Berkshire / Oxfordshire	3 / 3	13 / 10	69	
XII.	2d.	Gloucester	Glocestershire / Glocester / Herefordshire / Monmouthshire	2 / 1 / 2 / 2	22 / 3 / 8 / 8	123	
XIII.	3d.	Worcester	Shropshire / Staffordshire / Litchfield / Worcestershire / Worcester	2 / 2 / 1 / 2 / 1	16 / 15 / 1 / 10 / 3	135	
XIV.	WESTERN CIRCUIT. 1st.	Exeter	Cornwall / Devonshire / Exeter	3 / 3 / 1	12 / 22 / 1	105	
XV.	2d.	Salisbury	Dorsetshire / Poole / Hampshire / Southampton / Wiltshire	2 / 1 / 2 / 1 / 2	10 / 1 / 19 / 1 / 14	135	
XVI.	3d.	Wells	Somersetshire / Bristol	· 4 / 2	25 / 17		
XVII.		London	London	5	107	321	
XVIII.		London, &c.	Middlesex	5	296	888	
XIX.	WELSH DISTRICT. [g]	Chester	Cheshire / Welsh Counties at large [b] / Carmarthen [l]	3 / 12 / 1	16	48	
		Total of the Convicts for all the Districts		955[k]	2865[k]		

[c] The number in the Table is 66. See note [d].

[f] viz. for each Riding, two.

[g] The County of the City of *Chester* is in §. 3. p. 5. of the Bill among the jurisdictions included in the computation of the number of convicts for the *Welch* District: it is also specified in §. 5. p. 6. among the jurisdictions comprised within that District: but no Committee-Justices are allowed it by §. 6. The County of the Town of *Haverford-west* is in §. 3. p. 5. included in the computation of the average number of convicts for the *Welch* District: but it is not specified in §. 5. p. 6. among the jurisdictions comprised within that District: nor are any Committee-Justices allowed to it in §. 6.

[b] viz. for each, one.

[i] Blanks are left for these in the Bill: a column is here allotted to them for the convenience of any one who may choose to fill up the blanks with a pen, when those in the Bill are filled up.

[k] But see note [d].

[l] *Carmarthen* is among the jurisdictions included, &c. (See note [g]): but no Committee-Justices are allowed it.

PREFACE.

WHEN the propofed Bill, of which the enfuing Sheets are defigned to give a view, firft fell into my hands, I was employed in finifhing a work of fome bulk, in which I have been treating the fubject of *Punifhment* more at large. In that work I fhould have come in courfe to fpeak of the particular fpecies of Punifhment which is the fubject of this Bill. In that work, therefore, feveral of the obfervations would have come in courfe to be introduced, which I have here fubjoined to feveral parts of the text I have been abftracting: and being there digefted into a method, and forming a part of a fyftem, to which I have been giving that degree of regularity which it has been in my power to give it, would probably have come with more force, and fhewn

to

to more advantage, in company with the reft. On this account, had I been at liberty with refpect to time, I fhould rather have wifhed to have publifhed the whole together firft, before I had detached from it thefe fcattered fragments. The publication, however, of the propofed Bill in queſtion, with the intelligence that accompanied it, effectually precluded any fuch option. To have delayed the publication of this part of my principal work till the Bill had been brought in and paffed, would have been to delay it till that feafon had been over, in which, if in any, fuch parts of it as relate to the prefent fubject, promifed to be moft ufeful.

When I had read Mr. Howard's Book on Prifons, one fruit of it was, a wifh ftill more earneft than what I had been led to entertain from theory, to fee fome general plan of Punifhment adopted, in which folitary Confinement might be combined with Labour. This capital improvement (for as fuch I cannot help regarding it) in penal legiflation, I fat wifhing, with fcarce any mixture of hope, to fee carried into execution : for fome how or other the progrefs that had been already made in it near two

years

years ago in the Houſe of Commons *, had eſcaped me. How great then was my pleaſure and ſurprize at ſeeing a plan (which had already been pre-announced by the Judges in their circuits) originating, as appeared, from a high department in adminiſtration, and carrying with it every preſumption of its being adopted; in which, not only almoſt all the excellent matter of the book I have been ſpeaking of is engrafted, but many capital improvements ſuperadded? This incident gave me freſh alacrity, and ſuggeſted freſh deſigns.

This Bill (or draught of a Bill, as it is called in the title, not having been as yet brought into Parliament) is accompanied with a Preface, ſhort, indeed, but ample, maſterly, and inſtructive. In this preface an inſtructive but general idea is given of the theoretic principles upon which the plan of the Bill is grounded; and a more ample and detailed account of the documents which furniſhed materials and reaſons for the ſeveral proviſions of detail. A hiſtory of the ſteps that have been taken in the formation and proſecution of the plan is alſo interwoven.

---

* See Preface to the Bill, p. 5.

Upon this it will naturally enough be
afked, What was the occafion, and what can
be the ufe of the enfuing fheets? why pub-
lifh them? I anfwer—becaufe the Bill itfelf
is in fact *not* publifhed *:—becaufe, were it
publifhed, the contents of it are not quite fo
perfpicuous as I imagined they might be
made:—becaufe I hoped to be a means, in
fome degree, of forwarding the good purpofes of it, by ftating to the public more in
detail than it would have been competent
either to the text, or to the preface to have
done, the reafons on which the leading provifions in it feemed to be grounded, and
by fuggefting a few hints in the way of correction or addition.

" Not perfpicuous (I think I hear fome-
" body exclaiming) what Act of Parliament
" was ever more fo?" None, I muft confefs,
that I can think of: but this affords me no
reafon for retracting. The Legiflator, one
would indeed naturally fuppofe, might (and

---

* I mean in the fenfe ordinarily put upon the word
publifhed. It is not fold at any of the fhops. It has
no bookfellers nor printers name. It feems to have
been defigned for the perufal, not of the world at large,
but only of Members of Parliament, and of the Author's
private friends.

if he might, why fhould not he?) fpeak his own meaning fo plainly, that no one could fpeak it plainer; fo concifely, that no one could render his expreffion more concife: in fuch a method, both as to matter and form, that no one could caft it into a better. He might, one fhould think: for what fhould hinder him? Is he the lefs qualified for making himfelf underftood and remembered by being a legiflator? If he did, then, as he might do, expofitions would be ufelefs, and abridgements would be impracticable. But does he?—confult the twelve immenfe volumes of Acts of Parliaments: to which another is in the way to add itfelf every three years.

Let me not all this while be underftood to reflect cenfure on a great mafter of language, on whom nothing lefs than cenfure is intended. Had cuftom (that is the law of Parliament) left him at liberty to follow the dictates of his own intelligence, little or nothing, I fuppofe, would have been left to any one elfe to add to it on the fcore of perfpicuity: if (fuppofing the Bill and the Preface to come, as they purport to do, from the fame hand) it be reafonable to judge what he *could* have done from what he *has*

a 3   done.

done. On this head I have fcarce an idea
of making any greater improvement on his
draught than what he could have made, if
he had pleafed, and would, if he had
thought proper. He thought, I fuppofe (if
it occurred to him to propofe the fubject to
his thoughts) that one plan of reformation
was enough to proceed upon at once. On
the prefent occafion his bufinefs was to re-
form a part of the fyftem of punifhment
adopted by our legiflation : not to go about
reforming the legiflative ftile. He has therefore, of courfe, conformed, in a great meafure, to the ftile in ufe, though with a confiderable defalcation from the ufual complement of tautologies and redundancies : his
publication being a draught of the very in-
ftrument which it is intended fhould pafs
into an act.

The prefent abftract of it having no pre-
tenfions to be confidered in that light, I
have held myfelf at liberty to afford the reader many of thofe affiftances which parliamentary men, in all their authoritative pub-
lications, feem fo ftudious to reject.—I have
therefore prefixed numbers to the Sections :
I have given them marginal contents : I
have made frequent breaks in the letter-
prefs :

prefs: I have numbered, every now and
then, the leading articles, which, though included together in one Section, seemed to
claim each of them a separate measure of attention; and, by allotting to each a separate
line, have displayed them more distinctly
than if lumped together in one unbroken
mass. These, and other such typographical
affistances, are no more than what it is common enough for writers, on the moft ordinary fubjects, to give their readers: nor
would they be looked upon as fingular, or
indeed worth mentioning, but with refpect
to thofe intricate and important difcourfes
which ftand moft in need of them.

Another, and rather more ferious tafk has
been to break down the long fentences, into
which this compofition (being intended to
be paffed into an Act of Parliament) could
not but have been caft, into a multitude of
fhorter ones: to retrench the tautologies and
fuperfluities with which this compofition,
though remarkably fcanty on this head
(being intended for an Act of Parliament)
could not but abound. In the courfe of
thefe operations, I have here and there ventured to make fome little alteration in the
order of the feveral matters contained in the

fame

fame Section : but with entire Sections I
have no where taken the like liberty.

This abstract then (to mention a more
general use that may be made of it) will of
itself be sufficient to prove, that a sentence
of any given length is capable of being cast
into as many sentences, and, consequently,
that each sentence is capable of being made
as short, as there can be occasion to desire.
It is therefore of itself sufficient to divest the
long-windedness of our *legislative* (one may
say in general of our *legal*) stile, of the plea
of necessity, the only one which a man could
think of urging in its favour. Had this
been even my principal object, I should of
all others wished for a Bill like this to work
upon, for the same reason that grammarians
take the works of Pope, and Swift, and
Addison, for examples of solecisms in grammar *.

But to return. By the means above-
mentioned I will venture to hope, and that
without any pretensions to make it a ground
of vanity, that this abstract may be found to
read somewhat more pleasantly than even the
Bill itself : and that on this head the reader,

---

* See Bishop Lowth's Grammar, passim.

who

who means only to take a general view of
the Bill, and who is not in that line of duty
or of ftudy which would lead him to weigh
words and fyllables, may, as far as he thinks
he can depend upon the fidelity of this copy,
find it anfwer his purpofe as well as the original.

I am forry I cannot give equal fatisfaction
to his curiofity with refpect to the Preface ;
in which the elegance of a ftile, which is
the Author's own, has been at full liberty
to difplay itfelf, unfettered by technical forms
and prejudices.   This I muft not tranfcribe,
nor can prefume to imitate.   The uncouth
piles of parliamentary compofition have not
often been graced with fuch a frontifpiece.

Amongft other things we learn by it, is,
that " the difficulties which towards the end
" of the year 1775 attended the tranfpor-
" tation of convicts *," gave great weight to
the inducements, if they were not themfelves
the fole inducement, that led to the inftitution of this plan.   It may be fome confola-
tion to us, under the misfortunes from which
thofe difficulties took their rife, if they
fhould have forced us into the adoption of

---

* Page 1.

a plan

a plan that promiſes to operate one of the moſt ſignal improvements that have ever yet been made in our criminal legiſlation. It may not even be altogether extravagant to ſuppoſe, that at the end we may be found to have profited not much leſs than we ſhall have ſuffered by theſe misfortunes, when the benefits of this improvement come to be taken into the account. For let it be of ever ſo much conſequence that trade ſhould flouriſh, and that our property ſhould go on *encreaſing*, it ſeems to be of not much leſs conſequence that our perſons ſhould be ſafe, and that the property we *have* ſhould be ſecure. If then the efforts of our ſtateſ-men, to ſave the nation from the ſtroke of thoſe adverſities have not been attended with the ſucceſs they merited, let them not make it an excuſe to themſelves for ſinking into deſpondency. Let them rather turn their activity into a new channel: let them try what amends can be made, in ſome other line, to their own reputation, and to the public ſer-vice : let them look at home ; and if, after all that can be done, the nation muſt loſe ſomething in point of external ſplendour, let them try what they can gain for it in point of domeſtic peace.

I un-

I underftand that the plan is not yet looked upon as abfolutely compleated, which may be one reafon why the circulation of it has been hitherto confined to a few hands. The ample ufe, however, and liberal acknowledgement that has been made of the helps afforded by former volunteers, induced me to hope, that any lights that could be thrown upon the fubject, from any quarter, would not be ill received.

Whatever farther additions or alterations the propofed Bill may come to receive before it has been carried through the Houfe, there feems to be no great likelihood of their bearing any very great proportion, in point of bulk, to the main body of the Bill as it ftands at prefent. And as it is not yet clear but that it may be carried through in the courfe of this Seffions in its prefent ftate, it feemed hardly worth while to delay this publication in expectation of further materials that may either never come, or not in fuch quantity as to make amends for the delay. It will be an eafy matter, if there fhould be occafion, to give a fupplemental account of fuch new matter as may arife.

arife. The attention of the country gentlemen has already been drawn to the fubject by the general accounts given of the
plan by feveral of the Judges on their
circuits: and it fhould feem that no farther
apology need be made for giving as much
fatisfaction as can be given in the prefent
ftage of the bufinefs, to the curiofity which
a meafure, fo generally interefting, can fcarce
fail to have excited. That curiofity is likely
to be farther raifed by fome frefh enquiries,
which I underftand it is propofed to infti-
tute in the Houfe of Commons: and as the
refult of thefe enquiries comes to tranfpire,
the ufe and application of it will be the
better feen, by having fo much of the plan,
as is fketched out already, to refer to.

The hafte with which, on the above accounts, it was thought neceffary to fend the
enfuing fheets to the prefs, muft be my
apology for fome inaccuracies which, I fear,
will be difcoverable in them, as well in
point of method as of matter. It is not a
month fince the propofed Bill firft fell into
my hands in the midft of other indifpenfable
avocations.

The ufe of them, however, if they have
any, will, I hope, not be altogether con-

fined

fined to the short period between the publication of them, and the passing of the Bill
into a law. For when a great measure of
legislation is established, though it be too
firmly established to be in danger of being
overturned, it is of use, for the satisfaction of
the people, that the reasons by which it is
or may be justified, be spread abroad among
them.

Lincoln's-Inn,
March 28, 1778.

TABLE

TABLE I. CONTENTS

OF THE SECTIONS.

ADVERTISEMENT.

THE perſons who are ſtiled " *convicts*" in the enſuing abſtract, are ſtiled " *offenders*" in the propoſed Bill. I gave them the former name, to avoid a confuſion I found occur in ſpeaking of them, at times when there was occaſion to ſpeak of ſuch freſh offences as may come to be committed by the ſame perſons during their confinement, or of certain other offences which the Bill has occaſion to prohibit in other perſons.

In regard to *ſex*, I make, in general, no ſeparate mention of the *female*; that being underſtood (unleſs where the contrary is ſpecified) to be included under the expreſſion uſed to denote the *male*.

(marginal note:) " Con- " victs" put for " Offen- " ders,"

(marginal note:) Sex.

A VIEW

A

V I E W

O F T H E

HARD-LABOUR BILL.

THIS Bill has two capital objeets: 1ft, To provide a new eftablifhment of Labour-houfes all over England. 2dly, To extend and perpetuate the eftablifhment already fet on foot, for the confinement of convicts, to labour upon rivers. It confifts of fixty-eight Sections. The fifty-two firft are employed upon the former of the above objects: the feven following upon the latter: and the remaining nine upon certain cuftomary provifions of procedure and a few other matters that apply alike to both.

Firft with regard to the eftablifhment of Houfes of Hard Labour.—The firft twenty Sections are employed in making provifion

General view of the Bill.

B   for

2 A View of the Hard-Labour Bill.

for the erection of the buildings, and for the
appointment of the magiftrates and other officers to whom the management of that bufinefs is committed. The remaining thirty-
two Sections are employed chiefly in pre-
fcribing the regimen to be obferved in them
when built.

So much for the general out-line of this
regular and well-digefted plan. Let us now
take a view of the Sections one by one.

**Seft. I.
p. 1.
Preamble
—reafons
for the
bill.**

The firft Section, or Preamble, ftates the
general confiderations which determined the
author to propofe the eftablifhments in queftion. Thefe confiderations are the infuffi-
ciency of tranfportation for the purpofes of
example and reformation, the fuperior efficacy of a courfe of confinement and hard
labour, and the unfitnefs of the prefent
Houfes of Correction for that purpofe.

OBSERVATIONS.

**Difad-
vantages
of *Tranf-
portation*
in com-
parifon
with
*Hard La-
bour.***

Here would naturally be the occafion for a com-
mentator to dilate more particularly than it would
have been in character for the bill itfelf to have
done, upon the inconveniences of the old punifhment of tranfportation, which it meant to fuper-
fede, and the advantages of the new mode of punifhment, which it is the object of it to introduce.
This I fhall have occafion to do at large hereafter;
ftating in courfe the advantages and difadvantages

of

of each : but a flight and immethodical fketch is
as much as the prefent defign gives room for.

The punifhment of tranfportation, in its ordinary confequences, included *fervitude* ; the punifhment here propofed to be fubftituted in the room of
it. At all events, it included *banifhment*. Thefe two
it comprehended profeffedly and with defign ; befides an uncertain, but at any rate, a very afflictive
train of preliminary hardfhips, of which no account was taken ; amongft others, a great chance
of producing death.

Taking it all together, it had a multitude of bad
properties ; and it had no good ones, but what it
derived from fervitude, or are to be found in the
latter punifhment in a fuperior degree.

1. In point of proportion it was *unequal :* for a
man who had money might buy off the fervitude *.
With regard to the banifhment, it was again unequal ; for nothing can be more unequal than the
effect which the change of country has upon men
of different habits, attachments, talents, and pro-
penfities. Some would have been glad to go by
choice ; others would fooner die.

2. It was *unexemplary :* what the convicts fuffer-

---

* In virtue of the Statute 4 G. 1. c. 11. the Court
ufed to contract with fome perfon to convey the convict
to the place of deftination : thereupon the convict is
made over " to the ufe of" the contractor and " his
" affigns," who are declared in general terms to " have
" a property or intereft in" his " fervice," for the time
fpecified in the fentence.

Sect. I.
p. 1.

ed, were it much or little, was unknown to the people for whofe benefit it was defigned. It may be proved by arithmetic, that the purpofe of *example* is, of all the purpofes of punifhment, the chief.

3. It was *unfrugal* : it occafioned a great wafte of lives in the mode, and a great wafte of money in the expences, of conveyance.

4. It did anfwer indeed, in fome degree, the purpofe of *difabling* the offender from doing further mifchief to the community during the continuance of it ; but not in fo great a degree as the confinement incident to fervitude. It has always been eafier for a man to return from tranfportation, than to efcape from prifon.

5. It anfwered, indeed, every now and then, the purpofe of *reformation:* But by what means ? By means of the fervitude that was a part of it. It anfwered this purpofe pretty well ; but not fo well upon the whole, under the uncertain and variable direction of a private mafter, whofe object was his own profit, as it may be expected to anfwer under regulations concerted by the united wifdom of the nation, with this exprefs view.

Sect. II.
p. 2.
Labour-
Houfes
to be
erected
through-
out *Eng-
land* and
Wales.

Section II. provides in general terms for the erection of Houfes for the purpofes of confinement and labour throughout England and Wales. Thefe houfes are to be entirely feparate from all other public habitations, whether deftined for the cuftody or punifhment

ment of offenders, or for the maintenance of
the honeft poor. The legal appellation they
are directed to be called by, is that of *Houfes
of Hard Labour.*

OBSERVATIONS.

It might, perhaps, be as well to call them *Hard-
labour Houfes,* or *Labour-houfes,* at once. This,
or fome other equally compendious, is the name
that will undoubtedly be given them by the people
at large : the tendency of popular fpeech being to
fave words and fhorten names as much as poffible.
Such a name fhould be analogous to the names
Rafp-huys [Rafping-houfe] and *Spin-huys* [Spin-
ning-houfe] in ufe in Holland; and in fhort, to our
Englifh word *Work-houfe.* The technical name would
by this means be the fame as the popular. This
would, *pro tanto,* fave circumlocution, and guard
againft error in law proceedings. Where depart-
ing from the popular forms of fpeech is not neceffary, it is always inconvenient. So much for
an object, which, perhaps, may be thought to be
hardly worth the words that have been fpent upon
it.

Section III. is defigned to make provifion
for the raifing of the monies to defray the
charges of purchafing ground, and building :
and it prefcribes the proportions in which
fuch monies, when raifed, are to be diftributed among the diftricts eftablifhed in the

Sect. III.
p. 2.
Supplies
for build-
ing how
to be le-
vied and
diftri-
buted.

B 3　　　　　　　next

next section for the purpofes of the Act.* Thefe proportions it takes from the number of convicts that have been ordered for tranf-portation, in each county, within the compafs of a year, upon an average taken for feven years laft paft. A blank is left for the par-•ticular fund out of which the monies are to iffue,

OBSERVATIONS.

The contribution by which thefe monies are to be raifed, is made, we fee, not a local but a gene-ral one. A local tax, however, is that which feemed moft obvioufly to fuggeft itfelf, fince the expenditure is local : but a general one appears to be much preferable. Had the tax been local, it would have been raifed upon the plan of the county taxes : it would by that means have fallen exclu-fively upon houfeholders bearing fcot and lot. But the benefit of it, be it what it may, is fhared indifcriminately among the whole body of the peo-ple. Add to this, that the fums of money requi-fite for this purpofe will probably be large. Thefe, were they to be raifed at once in the feveral dif-tricts in the manner of a county tax, would be apt to ftartle the inhabitants, and prejudice them againft the meafure.

As to the proportion in which the fupplies are to

---

* See Table II. Col. 8.

be diftributed among the feveral diftricts, this is
taken, we fee, from the average number of convicts.
This was an ingenious way of coming at the
extent it would be requifite to give to the refpective
buildings, and the terms allotted would naturally be
proportioned to the extent. Rigid accuracy in
this apportionment, does not feem, however, to
have been aimed at. According to the method
taken, the allowance to the fmaller counties, will
be fomewhat greater in proportion than to the
larger. There are a great many counties whofe average number is fettled at *one:* the computation does
not defcend to fractions. This, if it be an error,
is an error on the right fide.

For two of the towns that are counties of themfelves, no average number of convicts, I obferve,
is ftated : thefe are, *Newcaftle upon Tyne* and *Haverfordweft.*

Upon turning to the table fubjoined to the bill,
it appears, that at *Haverfordweft,* there have been
no convicts at all within the time in queftion. At
Newcaftle upon Tyne the average is ftated at five.
The omiffion in the bill feems therefore to be
accidental.

Section IV. provides for the payment and
application of the monies mentioned in the
preceding Section. They are directed to be
paid to committees of Juftices, * or their
order, and applied to the building of the

* See Sect. VI.

Houfes

Sect. IV.
p. 6.
Houfes above-mentioned. The deficiencies, if any, in the provifion thus made, are to be borne afterwards by the diftricts.

Sect. V.
p. 6.
Counties
to be con-
folidated
into dif-
tricts.
By Section V. all England, including Wales, is caft, for the purpofes of this Act, into diftricts of a new dimenfion*. This divifion is made commenfurate to the divifion into circuits, as well as to that into counties. A certain number of thefe diftricts are included in each circuit: and each diftrict includes one or more counties. Towns, that are counties of themfelves, are put upon a footing in this refpect with counties at large. London and Middlefex form each a diftrict by itfelf. The whole principality of Wales, together with Chefhire and Chefter, are included in one diftrict. The whole number of diftricts is nineteen. The reafon it gives for this junction of the counties is, that it will ferve to leffen the expence.

OBSERVATIONS.

The circuit divifions, it feems, were thought too large; the county divifions too fmall; befides that, the latter are unequal. This is the cafe more particularly with the towns that are counties of them-

---

* See Table II. Col. 2. and 4.

felves,

felves, in comparifon with fome of the larger fhires. The ufe of making the diftricts lefs than the circuits, and at the fame time larger than the counties, is the adjufting the buildings to a convenient fize. An eftablifhment for the reception of a large number of perfons may be conducted, as the preambular part intimates, at a proportionably lefs expence than an eftablifhment for the reception of a fmall number. The ufes of making them lefs than the circuits, are two : 1ft, the leffening the expences of conveying the convicts from the place of trial to the place of punifhment: 2dly, the leffening the trouble and expence of the Juftices, who are to travel out of their own counties to the town where they are to meet to carry the act into execution. It is doubtlefs on the former principle that we are to account for the comprizing the twelve Welfh counties together with Chefhire and the city of Chefter, in one diftrict; for in this diftrict, extenfive as it is, the average number of convicts has been found to be lefs than in any other. On the two latter principles, it may feem rather inconvenient that this diftrict fhould be fo large. It is to be hoped, on this account, that the fituation chofen for the labour-houfe for this diftrict, will be as central as is confiftent in other refpects with convenience.

Sect. V.
p. 6.

Section VI. eftablifhes the Committees of Juftices who are to be appointed by the General Sefiions of their refpective counties, to meet together for the purpofes of carry-ing

Sect. VI.
p. 7.
Commit-
tees of
Juftices
to be ap-
pointed

for each diftrict by the Sef-fion.

ing this Act into execution at a particular place within each of the diftricts, within which their refpective counties are included*: and it fettles the proportion which the number of Committee-men in each county is to bear to the number of Committee-men in every other. Thefe Committees are empowered to appoint ftated meetings (giving ten days notice) and to make adjournments. The Committee-men are to be appointed at the next General Seffions after the paffing of this Act.

OBSERVATIONS.

The power of fending Juftices as Committee-men, is given, we may obferve, to all the counties at large, in various proportions, from one to five inclufive; likewife to all the town-counties except three; *Berwick*, *Chefter*, and *Haverfordweft*. Whether thefe omiffions are accidental or defigned, is more than I can take upon me to conjecture.

Sect. VII. p. 8. —or elfe by the *Cuftos Rotulorum.*

Section VII. provides againft any failure in the feffions to appoint Committee-men, or in the Committee-men to take upon them their office. If at the next General Seffions

---

* See Table II._Col. 5. and 3.

after

after the paſſing of the Act no Committee-men ſhould be appointed, or not enough, or if any ſhould refuſe, power is given to the *Cuſtos Rotulorum* to ſupply the deficiency within three months.

Sect. VII.
p. 8.

OBSERVATIONS.

This proviſion ſeems to proceed on the ſuppoſition, that in ſome places the meaſure of the bill may prove unpopular among the country magiſtrates. By way of a ſpur to them, this power is therefore given to the *Cuſtos Rotulorum* : but may it not be poſſible, eſpecially in ſome of the remote counties (ſuppoſe the Welſh counties) that even the *Cuſtos Rotulorum* may be tinctured with the local prejudices? It ſhould ſeem there could be no harm, rather than there ſhould be a gap in the execution of the Act, in ſubſtituting the *Lord Chancellor* to the *Cuſtos Rotulorum*, in the ſame manner as he is ſubſtituted to the Seſſions.

Section VIII. gives the Seſſions the power of changing their Committee-men from year to year : alſo of ſupplying vacancies at any time when they may happen.

Sect.
VIII.
p. 9.
—how to
be ſup-
plied or
changed.

OBSERVATIONS.

For conformity's ſake, might not this latter power, in default of the Seſſions, be given to the *Cuſtos Rotulorum?* and (if ſuch an addition were to be adopted) in his default, to the Lord Chancellor?

Section

Sect. IX.
p. 9.
Appoint-
ment of
clerks
and *trea-*
furers.

Section IX. requires the Committees to appoint each a *clerk* and *treasurer*, with such salaries as they shall think reasonable, removable at pleasure: the treasurer to give security in proportion to the sum likely to come into his hands *.

Sect. X.
p. 10.
Supplies
appropri-
ated.

Section X. appropriates the monies to be received by the Committees, or their treasurer, to the uses of the act.

Sect. XI.
p. 11.
Commit-
tees,
when and
where to
be held.

Section XI. appoints the place and time of the first meeting of the several Committees †; empowering them (after chusing their chairman, clerks, and treasurer) to adjourn to any other time and place within the same district. It then directs them, at this or any subsequent meeting, to make choice of a piece or pieces of ground to build on, one or more for each district. The orders for this purpose are to be certified in London and Middlesex to the King's-bench, and elsewhere to the Judges on their circuits; except that, in the Welch district, they are to be certified, not to any of the Welch Judges, but to those of Chester: in case of their disapproval, a second order is to be made, and

---

* See Table II. Col. 8.   † See Table II. Col. 3.

fo *toties quoties* : fo, alfo if the fpot pitched
upon be fuch as cannot be purchafed under
the powers given by the act *. With regard to the choice of the fpot it gives fome
directions. The Committees are required to
have regard to

  1. The healthinefs of the fituation.

  2. The facility of getting water.

  3. The *nearnefs* to fome trading town.

  4. But to avoid choofing any place
within a town, if any other convenient
place can be found.

  5. To give the preference to a place
furrounded with water, if in other refpects healthy and proper.

OBSERVATIONS.

With regard to the places of meeting it feems
rather extraordinary, that in the *Welfh* diftrict, a
place fo far from central as *Chefter*, fhould be
appointed. This obliges the whole body of Committee-men from *Wales* to travel out of their principality ; and a *Pembrokefhire* Juftice, who has to
traverfe all *North* and *South Wales*, may have, perhaps, near two hundred miles to go before he
reaches the place of his deftination. This inconvenience, indeed, is open, in fome meafure, to a

---

  * See Sect. XVII. and XX.

remedy,

remedy, by the power given to the Committees to choofe the place of their adjournment ; but at any rate, be the place ever fo central, in fo large a diftrict it cannot but be very remote from the abodes of the greater part of the Committee men. On this account, more efpecially if the *Welfh* diftrict is to remain undivided, might it not be proper to allow to the Committee-men, at leaft to fuch as had to travel out of their own counties, a fmall fum, (were it no more than ten fhillings a day,) to help indemnify them for their expences ? To many a magiftrate, who might, in other refpects, be better qualified for the bufinefs than a richer man, the expence (to fay nothing of the trouble) of making frequent journies to fuch a diftance as he might have occafion to travel to, might be an objection fufficient to prevent his acceptance of the office. There feems, at any rate, to be much more reafon for giving a falary to thefe Committee-men, than to perfons to be appointed Vifitors to the labour-houfes * ; fince the vifitors *may* be taken from the neighbourhood of the houfe, and the committee-men *muft*, many of them, come from a great diftance. Suppofe the allowance were to be fixpence a mile (the diftance to be afcertained by the oath of the traveller) and a fum not exceeding ten fhillings a day, fo long as the Committee continues fitting ?

The directions refpecting the choice of the fpot are well imagined, and ftrongly mark the judg-

---

* See Sect. XXII.

ment

ment and attention of the author. His ideas on this matter feem to quadrate pretty exactly with " the " fingular and well-directed refearches" (as he ftiles them) of Mr. Howard, to whofe merits, as a zealous and intelligent friend of human kind, it is difficult for language to do juftice. Sect. XI. p. 11.

One direction is, that a preference be given to a fpot furrounded with water, if it be in other refpects healthy and proper. Unlefs the water be *running* water, it is not very likely to be healthy.

Section XII. appoints a nominal proprietor, to whom the ground, when purchafed, is to be conveyed. This perfon is to be the town-clerk, for London; the clerk of the peace, for Middlefex; the clerk of affize of the circuit, for the other Englifh diftricts; with a blank left for the Welch; and for this purpofe the officers in queftion are refpectively conftituted bodies corporate. Sect. XII. p. 11. Ground to whom to be conveyed.

OBSERVATIONS.

After fuch a provifion, might it not be neceffary, or would it be fuperfluous, to provide that any action might be brought by the Committee in the name of any of the officers therein named, without naming the perfon who holds the office? This is a precaution taken in fome Acts. The occafion, if any, which may make it necefiary, is that of a vacancy happening in any of thofe of-

2   fices,

Sect. XII.
p. 11.

fices, at a time when it is requisite to bring (suppose) an action of trespass, for any encroachment or other trespass committed upon the spot thus to be made the property of the public. The trespass is committed (suppose) at a juncture that does but just admit of an action's being brought in such time as to be tried at the next assizes. The county is one of those in which the assizes are held but once a year. To obviate this difficulty, if there be one, why might not the Committee be impowered to bring any such action in their own name? in short, why might not the Committee themselves be the body corporate? This would save circuity; since whatever is done by the officer above mentioned, must be by their direction, and under their controul.

Sect.
XIII.
p. 12.
*Dimen-
sions* of
the build-
ings—*ac-
commoda-
tions.*

Section XIII. gives a proportion for determining the size of the several houses. They are to be large enough to contain *three* times the average number of convicts in a year, it being supposed that each convict will continue in them three years upon an average.

It likewise gives some directions with respect to the apartments. Each house, with its appurtenances, is to contain

      1. Lodging-rooms for the convicts.
      2. Storehouses and warehouses.
      3. An infirmary, with a yard adjoining.
      4. Several cells or dungeons.
      5. A chapel.

                               6. A

6. A burying-ground.
7. Apartments for the officers.

OBSERVATIONS.

To the above accommodations, it might, perhaps, be not amifs to add a *garden*, to fupply the
houfe with vegetables. The laborious part of the
work might be done by the prifoners themfelves,
who might be employed in it, either fome few of
them for a conftancy, or all of them occafionally.
In the later cafe, the privilege of being thus employed might conftitute an indulgence to be given
in the way of reward, as it would be an agreeable
relief from their ordinary domeftic labour *. It
feems probable, that a part of the labour might be
more oeconomically employed in this way than
upon the ordinary bufinefs of the houfe; even
though the prime coft of a wall to inclofe the
garden were taken into the account.

With regard to the " cells or dungeons," as
they are called, there are fome cautions that feem
highly neceffary to be obferved. That, for the
punifhment of the refractory, there fhould, in
every fuch houfe, be fome places of confinement,
under the *name* of dungeons, feems perfectly expedient: at the fame time that it is altogether in-
expedient there fhould any where be any place that

---

* Mr. Campbell, Superintendent of the Thames
convicts, employs a part of the ground he has the management of in raifing vegetables for their ufe.

C

fhould

should partake in all respects of the *nature* of those pestiferous abodes.

The purposes for which dungeons seem in general to have been calculated (I mean, such purposes as are justifiable) are two ; *safe custody*, and *terror*. The first must, in all cases, and the second may, in many cases, be desirable. But in aiming at these two purposes, another highly mischievous effect has unintentionally been produced; the exclusion of fresh air, and, as one consequence of it, the exposure of the room to perpetual damps. These apartments have been contrived underground ; hence there have been no lateral outlets ; but the entrance has been at top through a trap-door. By this means the air has remained almost continually unchanged : being breathed over and over again, it has soon become highly unfit for respiration : and having in a short time dissolved as much of the damp as it could take up, the remainder has continued floating without any thing to carry it off. The pernicious consequences of such a stagnation, in generating the most fatal and pestilential diseases, have been inferred from theory *, and have been but too fully verified by experience and observation †.

The business is then to make the necessary pro-

---

* See, with respect to the effects of air tainted with respiration, Priestly on Air, Vol. 1st and 2d. With respect to damps, Fordyce's Elements of the Practice of Physic, title *Catarrh*, and Hamilton's Essays.

† See Howard on Prisons, *passim*.

visions

vifions for the purpofes of fafe cuftody and terror, without excluding the frefh air. To effect the firft of thefe purpofes, other means in abundance are afforded upon the face of the bill, as it ftands at prefent (and if thefe be not fufficient, more might be afforded) by the ftructure and regimen of the prifon. Some expedients relative to this defign will be fuggefted in the courfe of thefe obfervations.

With regard to *terror*, the chief circumftance by which a dungeon is calculated to anfwer this purpofe, is the exclufion of day-light. In a dungeon this effect is produced by a conftant and unalterable caufe—the fubterraneous fituation of the place : but the fame effect may be produced more commodioufly, by means which might be applied or not, according as they were wanted ; and that without excluding the frefh air. The means I am fpeaking of are very fimple. Air travels in all directions ; light only in right lines. The light therefore may be excluded without the air, by adapting to the window a black fcuttle inflected to a right angle. If the door be made on the fide oppofite to the window, there will be as much draught as if the window opened directly into the air, without the fcuttle. Light might alfo be prevented from coming in at the door, by a return made to it in the fame] manner. By thefe means the prifoner's ordinary apartment, or any other apartment, may be made as gloomy as can be defired without being unhealthful.

I do not deny, but that the terrors of a dun-

geon

geon may depend in fome degree upon the circumftance of its being underground. In the
imaginations of the bulk of men, the circumftance of *defcent* towards the center of the earth is
ftrongly connected with the idea of the fcene of
punifhment in a future life. They depend in fome
meafure likewife upon the circumftance of *ftillnefs*; and the ftillnefs may at the fame diftance
from a founding body be made more perfect in a
dungeon than in an ordinary room : the uninter-
rupted continuity of the walls, at the fame time
that it excludes frefh air and day-light, ferving
alfo to exclude found. But I cannot look upon
the firft of thefe · circumftances of terror as
being of that importance, as to warrant the
paying fo dearly for it, as muft be paid by the
exclufion of wholefome air, which is fo apt to
change a punifhment, meant to be flight and temporary, into a capital one. As to the purpofe of
ftillnefs, it might be anfwered in a nearly equal
degree, by building cells (which, at any rate,
fhould be *called* dungeons) at a diftance from the
houfe. If the utmoft degree of ftillnefs were
thought not to be abfolutely neceffary to be infifted
on, a man's own lodging-room might at any time,
by the contrivance above mentioned, be fitted up for
the purpofe. On another account, however, the
lodging-rooms are not quite fo anfwerable to the
defign, as a place on purpofe, fince fomething of
the effect depends upon the *ftrangenefs* of the
place ; and upon its being known to be appropria-
ted to a penal purpofe.

After

After all, it does not seem adviseable to rest the whole of the punishment altogether upon the ground of terror; since terror is obliterated by familiarity. To make up a uniform complement of punishment, it is found necessary to have recourse to other circumstances of distress; such as the hard diet appointed by this bill. This consideration makes it the less necessary to be at any inconvenient expence in screwing the sentiment of terror up to the highest pitch.

Section XIV. directs, that as soon as a spot of ground shall have been purchased, advertisements shall be inserted by the Committees in the local news-papers, for builders to give in plans, with proposals and estimates; that a plan, when agreed upon by the Committee, shall be presented to the Judges as before; * and that after their approbation, signified in writing, the Committee may contract with the architect, and superintend the execution.

Sections XV. XVI. XVII. XVIII. and XIX. are taken up with a set of regulations, which, though very necessary, are collateral to the main purposes of the Act, being employed in giving the usual system of powers

---

* See Sect. 11.

requisite

requifite to effectuate purchafes to be made for public purpofes. With regard to thefe, it will be fufficient to give a very general fketch of the contents.

Sect. XV.
p. 13.
Difabilities to alien removed.

Section XV. removes the difabilities that proprietors of certain defcriptions lie under to alien.

Sect.
XVI.
p. 13.
Purchafe monies applied.

Section XVI. provides for the diftribution of the purchafe-money among the parties interefted.

Sect.
XVII.
p. 14.
Proprietors compelled.

Section XVII. prefcribes the ufual courfe for bringing unwilling proprietors to compliance.

Sect.
XVIII.
p. 15.
Price to be fettled by a jury.

Section XVIII. gives the ufual powers for fettling difputes concerning the value of the fpot, by the verdict of a jury.

OBSERVATIONS.

In fettling the fine to be impofed on witneffes in cafe of contumacy, it limits it, on the fide of diminution, to twenty fhillings, and on the fide of encreafe to ten pounds. This provifion feems liable to an inconvenience to which fines impofed by ftatute are very apt to be liable, that of the *punifhment's* proving, in many inftances, *lefs than equivalent to the profit of the offence.* A witnefs, we fhall

fay,

fay, knows of a circumftance, not notorious in its nature, that tends to diminifh the value of the land : or, let the circumftance be notorious, one witnefs alone is fummoned, his defign of failing not being fufpeﬁed. The value in queftion being the value of the fee fimple, it will be fomewhat extraordinary, if the difference made by fuch a circumftance, be not more than ten pounds. In fuch cafe, the owner, indemnifying the witnefs, is *fure* of gaining more than ten pounds, with only a *chance* of lofing a fum between ten pounds and twenty fhillings. A cafe might be figured, though not fo natural an one, in which either the witnefs or one of the parties might have an inducement to fupprefs a circumftance that tended to *encreafe* the value of the lands.

On the other fide, the danger is greater but the inconvenience lefs. The public does not fuffer fo much by a charge affecting the public purfe, as an individual by a lofs affecting his purfe to the fame amount.

Would there be any improper hardfhip in obliging the party in this cafe (as he is in fo many more cafes of greater inconvenience to him) to be examined upon oath ?

If proper evidence cannot be got at one time, it ought to be got at another. The trial therefore fhould be adjourned, or rather, to prevent private applications to the jurymen, a new trial fhould be appointed. Power fhould be given in fuch cafe to compel the appearance of the contumacious witnefs by arreft; and if at laft he appears and is

C 4   examined,

examined, the natural punifhment for his offence would be the being fubjected to the cofts of the preceding trial; fince, if any part of the charge were not borne by him by whofe delinquency it was occafioned, it muft fall upon fomebody who was innocent. This punifhment, however, ought to be open to mitigation in confideration of his circumftances; fince a charge to this amount, though it might be a trifle to one man, might be ruin to another.

In order, however, to ground a warrant for the apprehenfion of a witnefs who, on a former trial, had made default, an averment upon oath fhould be exacted, from the party on whofe behalf the warrant is applied for, that in his belief the perfon whofe teftimony is required is a material witnefs.

In juftice to the author, it may be proper, in this place, to obferve, that the deficiencies, if fuch they fhould be thought, which the above propofals are calculated to fupply, are not chargeable upon this bill any more than they are upon all the acts in the ftatute-book that have correfpondent paffages.

Sect.
XIX.
p. 16.
Cofts to
await the
verdict.
Sect. XX.
p. 17.
Saving for
dwelling-
houfes &
pleafure-
grounds.

Section XIX. provides, as is ufual, that the cofts of fuch a trial fhall await the verdict.

Section XX. makes a faving for dwelling-houfes and pleafure-grounds *.

So

---

* It would fave paper were the fix laft fections generalized

So much concerning the ground-plot and the buildings. Next come the provisions relative to the *regimen* of the Labour-houfes; thefe occupy the thirty-two following Sections, all but fix, from the thirtieth to the thirty-fifth inclufive, which concern the dif-, pofal of convicts, previous to the commencement of their punifhment.

Section XXI. provides, that when the houfes are ready, or nearly fo, the Committees fhall appoint officers, lay in ftock, and eftablifh regulations in the cafes not provided for by the Bill: with power at any time to make additions and alterations: every regulation to be approved of by the Judges afore mentioned.

Section XXII. enumerates the different claffes of officers to be appointed for each Labour-houfe: empowers the Committees to make removals and fupply vacancies, and to exact fecurity for the due execution of the refpective offices.

Thefe officers are to be,

---

ralized by an act on purpofe. The fame thing may be obferved refpecting a ftring of provifions at the end of the bill.

1. Two

1. Two visitors.

2. One governor.

3. One chaplain.

4. One surgeon or apothecary.

5. One storekeeper.

6. One task-master.

7. One gaoler.

8. " Such under-keepers, and other
" officers, as the Committee shall judge
" necessary."

Sect.
XXIII.
p. 18.
Governor
to have an
interest in
the work.
Section **XXIII.** respects the salary of the
governors : it directs that this salary shall be
so ordered by the Committee as to " bear a
" constant proportion to the quantity of la-
" bour performed in each house ;" and arise
chiefly, or, if possible, totally from that
source : and this to the end, that " it may
" become the *interest* as well as the *duty* of
" each governor to see that all persons un-
" der his custody be regularly and profitably
" employed."

OBSERVATIONS.

The principle here laid down as the ground of
the above provision, is an excellent lesson to legis-
lators, and is of more use in that view, than from
its seeming obviousness when announced, it might
at first appear to be. 'Tis owing to the neglect
of it, that we hear such frequent complaints of
the

the inexecution of the laws ; a misfortune ordinarily charged to the account of individuals;
but which ought in fact to be charged upon the
laws themfelves. The direction here given is
a happy application of that principle. It is by
ftrokes like thefe that genius and penetration
diftinguifh themfelves from fhallownefs and empi-
ricifm. The means that are employed to connect
the obvious intereft, of him whofe conduct is in
queftion, with his duty, are what every law has
to depend on for its execution. A legiflator, who
knows his bufinefs, never thinks it finifhed.while
any feafible expedient remains untried, that can
contribute to ftrengthen this connection. The
Utopian fpeculator unwarrantably prefumes, that a
man's conduct (on which fide foever his intereft
lie) *will* quadrate with his duty, or vainly regrets
that it will *not* fo.

The object in view in it, we fee, is partly
œconomical and partly *moral*; that fuch a profit
be drawn from the labour of the convicts as may
altogether, or at leaft in part, compenfate the expence of the eftablifhment ; and that the morals
of the convicts may be improved by a habit of
fteady and well-directed induftry. The means
by which it aims at the attainment of this object, are the giving to the perfon who has the
government of the convicts, an intereft in cauf-
ing the labour to be thus applied. This, as far as
it goes, is excellent; but perhaps there are means
by which the power applied to produce labour
might receive a ftill further encreafe. This
power

power can operate no farther than as it comes home to the perfons whofe labour is in queftion. Thefe perfons are the convicts.   Giving the governor an emolument in proportion to the labour they exert, it is expected, will caufe them to exert more labour than they would otherwife; why? becaufe the governor will employ fuch means as *he* has in his hands to induce them to exert it. Thefe means muft be either *punifhment* or *reward*; thefe being the only certain inducements by which one man can influence the conduct of another. Of thefe two inducements, punifhment is the moft obvious, and at firft view, the leaft coftly to him who is to apply them. Taken fingly, however, it is not always the moft efficacious, nor in the end the moft oeconomical. The quantity of work done will depend upon the ability of the workmen; the quantity of work which a tafk-mafter can exact by dint of punifhment, will depend upon the *apparent* ability of the workmen. Now, if the *apparent* ability of the workmen were always equal to the *real*, punifhment alone might be fufficient to extract from him all the labour he can exert.   But this is not the cafe: a man can always fupprefs without poffibility of detection, a great part of the ability he *actually* poffeffes, and ftifle in embrio all the further ftock of ability he *might* have poffeffed in future.   To extract, therefore, all the labour that can be got from him, it is neceffary to apply reward in aid of punifhment; and not only to punifh him for falling fhort of the *apparent* meafure of his ability,

but

but to reward him for exceeding it. Thus it is, that the courfe which recommends itfelf to *fenti-ment*, as the moft humane, approves itfelf to *rea-fon* as the moft ufeful.

It feems, therefore, as if it might be an ufeful fupplement to the above provifion, if the convicts themfelves were to be allowed fome profit, in proportion to the produce of their own labour. This profit fhould be the *grofs* profit ; becaufe that depends upon themfelves ; not the clear profit, becaufe that depends upon the oeconomy of the governor. Such a provifion would have a double good effect, on the welfare of the public at large, in making their labour more productive ; and on their own happinefs, by making them take a pleafure in their bufinefs.

It is to be obferved, however, that this regulation can have effect only in the cafe where the produce of the labour of one man can be diftinguifhed from that of the labour of another. From a paffage in fection 27th, it looks as if the notion of the author were, that it could be done in all kinds of manufactures. But this, I fear, is hardly the cafe. If not, would it or would it not be worth while to reftrict the employment of the convicts to fuch manufactures in which it *could* be done ? Where it cannot, the profit that each man can reap from his own labour will be leffened in proportion as the number of his comrades is encreafed. To illuftrate this,

Let

Sect.
XXIII.
p. 18.

Let the value of the grofs produce of each man's labour be, upon an average, } by the day { d. 6 } that is, by the week { s. 3

Let the profit allowed him be one-fixth, } that is, by the day { d. 1 } that is, by the week { d. 6

If he has five comrades, whofe work is blended indiftinguifhably with his own, fo that there are fix perfons in all to fhare the profit of his labour, his fhare will be but one-fixth of that one-fixth, that is, } by the day { $\frac{1}{6}$ of 1 d. } by the week { d. 1

He fhares, it is true, in the profit upon their labour; but over this he has not that command that he has over his own. He knows, therefore, that he cannot depend upon it. If he could depend upon it, it would not be worth his while to exert his own.

A queftion

A queſtion that occurs here is, in what manner ſhall the workman be let in to participate of the profits ? ſhall he be enjoined a certain taſk without profit, and then be allowed the whole profit upon the overplus ? or, ſhall he be enjoined a leſs taſk, and then be allowed a ſhare only in the profit upon the overplus ? or, ſhall he be allowed a ſhare, but of courſe a leſs ſhare, upon every part of the produce of. his labour, be it leſs or more ? All theſe three expedients appear to be practiſed in different foreign work-houſes. The firſt (or poſſibly the ſecond) in the great houſe of correction at *Ghent* * ; the ſecond, in the houſe of correction at *Delft* in Holland † ; the third, in the great houſe of correction in Hamburgh ‡. The firſt, however, is liable to this objection ; if the taſk be ſuch, as any man of the leaſt degree of adroitneſs can perform, it muſt to ſome of the moſt adroit, be a very ſlight one ; to ſuch perſons the reward will be a very laviſh one ; more certainly than is neceſſary, perhaps more than is expedient. If it be ſuch as require more natural adroitneſs than falls to the ſhare of every body, ſome will be altogether excluded from the reward. The ſecond expedient too, will, in a greater or leſs degree, be liable to the one or the other of theſe objections. The third is free from both : this, therefore, ſeems to be the preferable one of the three.

---

* See Howard 143.   † Ib. 132.

‡ Ib. 116.

As

As to the making the emoluments of the governor bear a conftant proportion to the quantity of
labour, the beft way feems to be to give him fo
much *per cent.* upon the produce of it, at the fame
time enfuring it not to fall fhort of fuch or fuch
a fum ; fuppofe one hundred pounds a year.   The
fum it is thus infured at, muft, on the one hand,
be *as much* as is requifite to induce a competent
perfon to undertake the charge : on the other hand,
it muft *not* be fo much as appears likely to come
near the probable profit that might be made from
the *per* centage upon the produce of the labour.
If this profit were to be lefs than the falary allowed in lieu of it, or indeed, if it were but
little more, it would not make it worth his while
to beftow the trouble it might take him to improve
that fund to the beft advantage.

Sect.
XXIV.
p. 18.
Eftablifh-
ment of
officers
how va-
riable.

Section XXIV. gives power to the Committees to " encreafe, diminifh, difcontinue,
" or vary the number of officers," with the
approbation of the judges as before; " ex-
" cept by taking away or difcontinuing the
" offices of

" 1. Vifitor.
" 2. Governor.
" 3. Chaplain.
" 4. Surgeon or apothecary."

OBSERVATIONS.

Poffibly the meaning might have been more

clearly

clearly expreſſed by giving the power to ſuppreſs any of the officers mentioned in ſection 22d, (except as herein is excepted) or create any new ones, or alter the number of officers in each office. Thus ample, at leaſt, I take the powers to have been, that were meant to be conferred.

Section XXV. eſtabliſhes the œconomical powers of the governor.

1. It conſtitutes him a body corporate.

2. It empowers him to contract for the articles wanted in the houſe: to wit,

　1. For cloathing, diet, and other neceſſaries, for the uſe of the convicts.

　2. For implements and materials of any manufacture they may be employed in.

3. It empowers him to carry on ſuch manufacture, and to ſell the produce.

4. It impowers him to draw on the treaſurers of the ſeveral counties included within the diſtrict, for the amount of the above expences.

5. Alſo for the other expences of the houſe, under the following heads, *viz.*

　1. Salaries.

　2. Wages.

　3. Coroner's fees.

　4. Funeral charges.

D　　　　5. Re-

5. Repairs.

6. Other neceffaries in general.

6. It impowers him to draw for the firft quarter in advance: fuch draught being allowed by the Committee, and counter-figned by their clerk.

7. Laftly. Whatever monies he receives as above, it enjoins him to apply to the purpofes for which they are iffued.

OBSERVATIONS.

It could hardly have efcaped the notice of the author, to what a degree the power of making thefe contracts lies open to abufe ; and yet, upon the face of the claufe now before us, this power is committed folely to the governor, without any exprefs reference to the Committee for their con-currence. The danger, however, is not altoge-ther unprovided againft. They have a general power of difplacing him ; and the dependance feems to have been upon their availing themfelves of that power to exercife an occafional negative upon thefe contracts, or to make fuch general regulations they fhould deem requifite to obviate the abufe.

Sect.
XXVI.
p. 19.
Expences
how to be
appor-

Section XXVI. proportions the fum to be drawn for upon each county, &c. within the diftrict, to the average number of the con-

victs

victs, as declared in Section 8*. Disputes
concerning the proportions it refers to the
Judges, as before †, whose determination it
makes final.

Section XXVII. prescribes the accounts
that are to be kept by the governor, store-
keeper, and task-master.

1. The governor is directed to enter into
a book " all accounts touching the maintenance of the house, and the convicts therein."

2. The governor and storekeeper are each
to keep separate accounts of all the stock
brought into the house.

3. The store-keeper is to deliver out the
stock to the task-master, and take receipts
from him.

4. The task-master is to deliver out the
work to the convicts.

5. The task-master is to keep accounts of
the quantities daily worked by them respectively.

6. He is to return the materials, when
wrought, to the store-keeper, taking his receipt for them.

7. He is to dispose of the wrought materials, with the privity of the governor, to

Sidenotes:
tioned among the coun- ties.

Sect. XXVII. p. 20. Accounts to be kept.

---

* See Tab. II. Col. 5.   † See Sect. 11, 21.

whom

whom he is to pay the produce: for which the governor is declared to be accountable to the Committee.

8. The governor and store-keeper are to keep separate accounts of the materials wrought and disposed of under the following heads:

    1. Species and quantity of the materials in question.

    2. For what sold.

    3. When sold.

    4. To whom sold.

Section XXVIII. directs the manner in which the above accounts shall be audited by the Committee:

1. They are to examine the entries, to compare them with the vouchers, to verify them by the oaths of the governor and store-keeper, and upon that to allow or disallow them.

2. An account, if allowed, is to be signed by two or more members of the Committee.

3. If the balance should be in favour of the governor, they are to pay him by draughts in the manner above set forth *: if

---

* See Sect. XXV.

against

Sect.
XXVIII.
p. 21.

againſt him, they may either leave it in his hands, or order it to be paid over as they think proper.

Sect.
XXIX.
p. 21.
Their
power as
auditors.

Section XXIX. empowers the Committee, in caſe of their ſuſpecting fraud, to examine upon oath any perſons whatſoever reſpecting the above accounts; and in caſe of any falſe entry, or fraudulent omiſſion, or other fraud, or any colluſion of an officer or ſervant with any other officer or ſervant, or with any other perſon, to diſmiſs the officer or ſervant, and appoint another: or, if they think fit, to indict the offender at the next Seſſions of the Peace for the place wherein the houſe is ſituated: and it limits the puniſhment to a fine not exceeding ten pounds, or impriſonment not exceeding ſix months, or both: ſaving the right of action to any party injured.

OBSERVATIONS.

With reſpect to the puniſhment of officers, this ſection, when compared with ſection 24, ſeems not altogether free from ambiguity. After impowering the Committee to diſmiſs officers for miſbehaving in any of the manners ſpecified, it goes on and ſubjoins, in the disjunctive, another mode of puniſhment; they may be diſmiſſed, it ſays, " *or* " indicted. It looks, from hence, as

D 3   if

if it were not the intention of the author, that
an offender of the defcription in queftion fhould
be punifhed by difmiffion and indictment both;
yet this he might be, notwithftanding, under the
general power of difmiffion at pleafure, given by
fection 24; unlefs this fection be underftood *pro
tanto* to repeal the other.

It may be faid by way of reconciling the two
fections, that the fenfe is, that the offender may,
if thought proper, be difmiffed, or he may be indicted; but that if he has been difmiffed, he is
not to be indicted.   But fuppofe him to have
been *indicted firft*, and perhaps convicted, may
he, or may he not then afterwards be *difmiffed?*

As to the *quantum* of punifhment allowed to be
inflicted upon indictment, this may, perhaps,
be liable, though in a much inferior degree, to
the objection againft a correfpondent provifion
ftated in fection 18.

With refpect to the jurifdiction within which
the indictment is to be preferred, may there not
be fome danger in confining it to the feffions of
the peace for the very place within which the
houfe is fituated? Suppofe the delinquent to be a
governor, and the houfe to be fituated in a fmall
town, fuch as *Warwick* or *Wells* *; the houfe at
Warwick is calculated for 118 convicts; that at
Wells for 126. The contracts for the maintenance of the houfe are all to be made by the governor; might not this privilege give him a con-

* See Table II. Col.

fiderable

fiderable degree of influence among the grand jurymen for fuch fmall places as thofe towns. There are no feparate feffions indeed for *Wells* or *Warwick*; fo that the grand jurymen at the feffions there, would come out of the body of the county. But it might very well happen, on any given occafion, that the grand juries for the refpective counties might, the greater part of them, come out of thofe towns; and the towns of *Lincoln, Norwich, Durham, York, Gloucefter, Worcefter, Exeter,* and *Chefter,* all of them places wherein the Committees are to meet, and within which therefore Labour-houfes are likely enough to be fituated, have all feparate feffions of their own. The houfes, indeed, are directed not to be " *within* " any town, if any other convenient place can " be found;" that is, not encompaffed with buildings; but this may not every where hinder their being within the jurifdiction : nor is the direction peremptory; and they are recommended to be *near* a town, to wit, a town of trade. The danger certainly is not very great; but it may be obviated without difficulty. All that is neceffary is, to impower the Committee, if they think fit, to prefer the indictment in any adjoining county at large; or in London or Middlefex, if the diftrict be in the home circuit.

Sect. XXIX, p. 21.

Section XXX. declares for what offences, and for what terms, convicts may be committed to thefe houfes. Thefe are

Sect. XXX. p. 22. Convicts what, when and for what

D 4

For

terms to
be com-
mitted to
thefe
houfes.

For petty larceny, $\left\{\begin{array}{l}\text{any term not exceed-}\\\text{ing two years.}\end{array}\right.$

For offences punifhable by tranfportation, $\left\{\begin{array}{ll}\text{for 7 years} & \left\{\begin{array}{l}\text{any term not}\\\text{exceeeding } 5\\\text{years, nor lefs}\\\text{than 1 year.}\end{array}\right.\\[2em]\text{for 14 years} & \left\{\begin{array}{l}\text{any term not}\\\text{exceeding } 7\\\text{years.}\end{array}\right.\end{array}\right.$

Offenders are to be fent to the houfes as foon as the Committee certifies to the *judges*, as before *, that the houfe is ready to receive them.

Sect.
XXXI.
p. 23.
—how to
be dif-
pofed of
till the
houfe is
ready.

Section XXXI. empowers the feveral courts in the mean time, until the Labour Houfes are made ready, to commit offenders to the *County Bridewells*, injoining the Juftices in Seffions to fit up thofe places for the " temporary reception, fafe cuftody, " employment, and due regulation of the offenders" that are to be fent there: and it declares that for fuch time the places in queftion fhall be deemed Labour-houfes, for

---

* See Sect. 11, 21, 26.

all

all the purposes within the meaning of this Act.

Section **XXXII.** is confined to *male* convicts. It empowers Courts to commit offenders of the male sex to work upon the Thames, or upon any other river that may be fixed upon for that purpose by an order of council. These are to work under the direction of a superintendant: to be appointed, for the Thames, by the Justices of Middlesex; for any other river, by the Justices of such adjoining counties as shall be fixed upon by the privy council.

Sect.
XXXII.
p. 24.
—what
to be or-
dered to
hard la-
bour up-
on rivers.

The terms for which they may be committed are } not to be less than } 1 year, nor to exceed } 7 years.

The provisions of this Section are in the preambular part of it declared to be designed " for the more severe and effectual " punishment of *atrocious* and daring of- " fenders."

OBSERVATIONS.

The confinement and labour upon the Thames is looked upon, it appears from this, as being severer than

Sect.
XXXII.
p. 24.

than the confinement and labour is at prefent in the
county bridewells, or, is expected to be in the Labour-houfes in queftion. It is not exprefsly referred to the option of the courts, which of thefe
two fpecies of hard-labour or confinement they
will order a man to: but as, by feparate claufes,
they are impowered to order a convict of the defcription in queftion to each, and not peremp-to-
rily enjoined to order him to either; it follows of
neceffity, that it was meant they fhould have that
option. The preambular words above quoted being too loofe to operate in the way of *command,*
can be intended only for *direction.*

With regard to the fuprintendent under whofe
management the Thames convicts are to be, it
fpeaks of him as one who is *to be* appointed by the
Middlefex Juftices. Now, the prefent act under
which the prefent fuperintendent *has* been appointed, is, by the laft fection of the bill to be repealed. This being the cafe, it looks as if a frefh
appointment of the fame or fome other perfon to
be fuperintendent would be neceffary, unlefs fome
flight alteration were made in the wording of this
claufe.

Sect.
XXXIII.
p. 24.
Provifo
for con-
victs par-
doned on
condi-
tion.

Section XXXIII. extends the provifions refpecting convicts fentenced to tranfportation,
to capital convicts pardoned on that condition: and it allows and enjoins any one Judge,
before whom the offender was tried, upon
a written notification of his Majefty's mercy, given by a fecretary of ftate, to allow the
offender

offender the benefit of a conditional pardon, as if it were under the Great Seal.

Sect. XXXIII. p. 24.

Section XXXIV. prescribes the method in which an offender is to be conveyed from the place of sentence to the place of punishment, together with the documents by which the right of conveying him thither, and keeping him there, is to be established.

Sect. XXXIV. p. 25. —how to be conveyed, and under what certificate.

Upon the making of any order for the commitment of an offender to hard-labour, a certificate is to be given by the clerk of the court to the sheriff or gaoler who has him in custody.

In this certificate are to be specified,

1. The Christian name of the offender.
2. His sur-name.
3. His age.
4. His offence.
5. The court in which he was convicted.
6. The term for which he is ordered to hard-labour.

Immediately after the receiving such certificate, the gaoler is to cause the offender to be conveyed to the place of punishment, and to be delivered, together with the certificate, as the case is, •to the governor or superintendent, or " such person or persons

" as

" as fuch governor or fuperintendent fhall
" appoint :" and the perfon who receives
him is to give a receipt in writing, under
his hand : which receipt is declared to be a
fufficient difcharge to the perfon who deli-
vers him. This certificate " the governor
" or fuperintendent, or other perfon or per-
" fons to whom fuch offender fhall be fo
" delivered," is required " carefully to pre-
" ferve."

OBSERVATIONS.

With refpect to the words, " fuch perfon or per-
" fons as fuch governor or fuperintendent fhall ap-
" point," I doubt fome little difficulty may arife.
Does the paffage mean any perfon in general acting
under the governor or fuperintendent ? any perfon
employed by them as a fervant in the difcharge of
the duties of their office ? or does it mean, that
fome one particular perfon or perfons fhould be
appointed by them for this particular purpofe ; fo
that a delivery made to any other perfon in their
fervice fhould not be good ? On the one hand, it
is not every perfon who may be occafionally employed in the fervice, whom it would be fafe to
truft with fuch a charge : on the other hand, it
might be attended with a good deal of inconvenience, if upon any occafion the governor or fuperintendent, and any one perfon refpectively appointed by them for this purpofe, fhould by any
accident be both abfent or difabled by illnefs. A

remedy

remedy to both inconveniencies may be the directing the governor to give standing authorities for this purpose in writing, to such a number of his servants, as may obviate any danger there might be of their being all out of the way at the same time. In such case, there could be no inconvenience in making it necessary to the discharge of him who is to deliver the prisoner, that he who is to receive him, shall have produced and shewn him such authority.

Sect.
XXXV.
p. 26.
Charges
of con-
veyance.

Section XXXV. provides for the fees and expences of conveyance. The clerk of the court, on granting the certificate, and the sheriff or gaoler, on delivering the offender, are to have the same fees as would respectively have been due to them had he been " sentenced to" transportation.

The expence of those fees, and the other expences of conveyance, are to be borne by the jurisdiction over which the court presides; and are to be paid by the clerk of the court, upon an order made by the General Sessions of the peace for the jurisdiction.

Sect.
XXXVI.
p. 26.
Gover-
nors and
Superin-
tendents,

Section XXXVI. appoints, in general terms, the powers a governor or superintendent, or persons acting under them, are to have, and the punishments they are to be liable

liable to in caſe of miſbehaviour : thoſe powers and theſe puniſhments it declares to be the ſame as are incident to the office of a ſheriff or gaoler.

Section XXXVII. gives directions reſpect- ing the ſpecies of work in which the con- victs are to be employed. For this purpoſe it marks out two claſſes of employments, correſpondent to ſo many different degrees of bodily ſtrength. Thoſe whoſe ſtrength is in the firſt degree, whether of the one ſex or the other, it deſtines to labour of the " hardeſt and moſt ſervile kind:" thoſe whoſe ſtrength is in a lower degree, to " leſs laborious employments:" and in de- termining whether an offender ſhall be deemed to come under one of theſe claſſes or another, it directs that the three circum- ſtances of *health*, *age*, and *ſex*, be all taken into conſideration.

Of each of theſe claſſes of employment it gives examples. Of the hardeſt and moſt ſervile kind it propoſes,

1. Treading in a wheel.

2. Drawing in a capſtern for turning a mill, or other machine or engine.

3. Beating hemp.

4. Raſping logwood.

8

5. Chopping

5. Chopping rags.
6. Sawing timber.
7. Working at forges.
8. Smelting.

Of the lefs laborious clafs, it inftances:

1. Making ropes.
2. Weaving facks.
3. Spinning yarn.
4. Knitting nets.

Of thefe, and other fuch employments, it leaves it to the Committees, to ˙choofe fuch as they fhall deem moft conducive to the profit, and confiftent with the convenience, of the diftrict.

Section XXXVIII. regulates the lodgment of the offenders.

1. The males are at all times to be kept " feparate from the females; without the " leaft communication on any pretence " whatfoever."

2. Each offender is in all cafes to have a feparate room to fleep in.

3. Each offender, as far as the nature of his employment will admit, is to work apart from every other.

4. Where the nature of the employment requires two perfons to work together, the

room

room they work in is directed to be of
" suitable dimensions."

5. Such two persons shall not continue
together but during the hours of work.

6. Nor shall the same two persons work
together for more than three days succef-
sively.

7. If the nature of the work requires
" many" to be employed together, " a com-
" mon work-room or shed" may be allotted
them.

8. But in this case the governor, or some-
body under him, " shall be constantly pre-
" sent to attend to their behaviour."

9. If the work require instruction, in-
structors shall be provided, who shall be
paid by the Committee.

It likewise gives some directions concerning the dimensions and structure of
the lodging-rooms.

1. They are
not to *exceed* in
{ length { twelve feet.
{ breadth { eight ditto.
{ height { eleven ditto.

2. They are to have no window within
six feet of the floor.

OBSERVATIONS.

Nothing can be better contrived than this
little string of regulations. They appear to be
                                          such

Sect.
XXXVIII.
p. 27.

be fuch as cannot but be conducive in the higheft degree to the two great purpofes of fafe cuftody and reformation. They involve, it is true, a very confiderable degree of expence ; but perhaps there is no cafe in which there is more to be faid in behalf of a liberal fupply.

With regard, indeed, to the firft of the above reftraints, this, it muft be confeffed, is of itfelf, in fome cafes, a pretty fevere, and upon the whole, rather an unequal punifhment. The amorous appetite is in fome perfons, particularly in the male fex, fo ftrong, as to be apt, if not gratified, to produce a ferious bad effect upon the health : in others, it is kept under without diffi-culty. On the fcore of punifhment, therefore, this hardfhip, could it be avoided, would, on account of its inequality, be ineligible. Under a religion which, like the Mahometan or Gentoo, makes no account of the virtue of continence, means, perhaps, might be found not inconfiftent with the peace of the fociety, by which thefe hardfhips might be removed. But the Chriftian religion, at leaft according to the notions enter-tained of it in proteftant countries, requires the temporal governor to put an abfolute negative upon any expedients of this fort. Since then the grati-fication of this defire is unavoidably forbidden, the beft thing that can be done is, to feclude the parties, as much as poffible, from the view of every object that can have a tendency to foment it. On this account, the firft of thefe regulations is as ftrongly recommended by humanity as a means

E   of

of preferving the quiet of each individual convict, as it is by policy as a means of preferving the peace of the whole community of them at large. Happily the difpofitions of nature in this behalf feconds, in a confiderable degree, the difpofitions of the legiflator. Hard-labour, when not compenfated by nourifhing and copious diet, has a ftrong tendency to diminifh the force of thefe defires, whether by diverting the attention, or by diminifhing the irritability of the nervous fyftem, or by weakening the habit of body : and the defire, when the habit of gratifying it is broken off, fubfides and becomes no longer troublefome.

With regard to the fize of the rooms, this we fee has limits fet to it on the fide of augmentation; on the fide of diminution it has none. This partial limitation, I muft confefs, I do not very well perceive the reafon of. Errors, if at all, feem more to be apprehended on the fide of diminution than on that of augmentation. That the rooms fhould not be lefs than of a certain fize, is conducive to health. The danger feems to be, leaft the committees fhould, out of oeconomy, be difpofed to put up with narrower dimenfions. If the fums provided by the bill out of the national fund are not fufficient, the deficiency, we may remember, is to be provided for by the counties.

Section XXXIX. prefcribes the *times* of work.

1. The days of work are, unlefs in cafe
of

of ill health, to be all days in the year:
except

    1. All Sundays.

    2. Chriftmas-day.

    3. Good-Friday.

2. The hours of work, as many as day-
light and the feafon of the year will permit,
including two intervals : *to wit*

    1. For breakfaft - - - Half an hour.

    2. For dinner - - - One hour.

3. At the clofe of the day, when working-
time is over, fuch of the materials and implements as admit of removal, are to be
removed from the work-rooms to places
proper for their fafe cuftody, there to be
kept till it comes round again.

OBSERVATIONS.

With refpect to the hours of work, the duration of day-light, if taken for the fole meafure,
(as one would fuppofe it to be by this paffage in
the bill) would, I doubt, be found rather an inconvenient one. In the depth of winter, the time
of working can fcarcely begin fo early as eight
in the morning, nor continue fo late as four in
the afternoon. In the height of fummer, it
may begin earlier than three in the morning, and
it may continue later than nine in the evening ;
but if from eight till four, that is eight hours, be

enough,

enough, from three to nine, that is sixteen hours,
were even nothing more than the *duration* of the
labour to be considered, is surely too much. But
labour of the same duration and intensity, is severer
in summer than in winter : heat rendering a man
the less able to endure it. The better way, therefore, seems to be, if not to make the time of working longer in winter than in summer, at least to
make it of an equal length. As eight hours, or
the least time of day-light, therefore, is evidently
too short a time, this will make it necessary to
have recourse to lamps or candles. As the walls
and floors will of course be of brick or stone,
without any combustible linings, these artificial
lights can scarcely be attended with any danger.

Whatever be the hours of labour fixed upon as
most proper for an average, there are some among
the employments above mentioned *, that will
probably be found too laborious for a man to be
confined to during the whole time. In such a
case, either he must remain without any thing to
do, or employed in some kind of work so much
less laborious as to serve as a kind of relaxation
from the other. The latter course seems beyond
comparison the best. On this account, it seems
as if it would be of advantage, that no person
should be confined exclusively to the most laborious of the classes of employments above specified;
but that such offenders as were destined principally
to an employment of that class should, for some
part of the day, be turned over to one of the se-

---

* See Sect. XXXVII.

dentary

dentary kind. On the other hand, neither would it be fo well, perhaps, that offenders of the leaft robuft clafs fhould be confined wholly to employments purely fedentary. The relief of the former and the health of the latter would, it fhould feem, be beft provided for by a mixture of the laborious and the fedentary. By this means, the time of the convicts might, it fhould feem, be better filled up and the total quantity of their labour rendered more productive.

The great difficulty is, how to fill up their time on Sundays : for, with regard to men in general, more particularly to perfons of this ftamp, the danger always is, that if their time be not filled up, and their attention engaged, either by work or by innocent amufement, they will betake themfelves either to mifchief or to defpondency. Divine fervice, it is true, is appointed to be performed, and that twice a day ; but that, according to the ordinary duration of it, will not fill up above four hours ; that is, about a quarter of the day.

To fill up the remainder, four expedients prefent themfelves. 1. One is, to protract the time of reft for that day; which may be done either by letting them lie longer, or fending them to bed earlier.

Another is, to protract the time of meals.

A third is, to protract the time of divine fervice.

A fourth is, to furnifh them with fome other kind of employment.

E 3
The

The two firſt are commonly enough practiſed by the working claſs of people at large who are at liberty. But when put both together, they will not go any great way.

, The time of attendance at church might be lengthened in two ways. 1. By adding to the ordinary ſervice a ſtanding diſcourſe or diſcourſes particularly adapted to the circumſtances of the congregation. This might confiſt, 1ſt, of prayers, 2dly, of thankſgivings; neither of which, however, could, with propriety, be very long; and 3dly, of a diſcourſe compoſed of moral inſtructions and exhortations. The inſtructions and exhortations would naturally have two objects; the conduct of the hearers, 1ſt, during the continuance of their puniſhment: 2dly, after their reſtoration to ſociety.

2. Another way of adding to the church ſervice is by *muſic.* This will, at any rate, be a very agreeable employment to many; and, if properly managed, may be a very uſeful one to all; even to thoſe who have no natural reliſh for muſic in itſelf. The influence which church-muſic has over the generality of men in bringing them to a compoſed and ſerious turn of mind is well known. The muſic might be either vocal only or aſſiſted by an organ. In either caſe, the vocal part might, with a little inſtruction, be performed by the congregation themſelves; as it is at the Magdalen, and other public foundations.

4thly, As to other employments, *walking* (in as far as their limits will permit them) might go
                                                        ſome

Sect.
XXXIX.
p. 28.

some way towards filling up their time. This
would be an additional use for the garden pro-
posed in the observations to section 13. On this
occasion, to prevent insurrections and cabals, the
convicts might be connected two and two together; a slight chain, not heavy enough to incom-
mode them by its weight, might answer the purpose: each offender would, by this means, be a
clog and a spy upon his companion. In this
view, the idea adopted in section 38, with regard to the manner of working, might be pursu-
ed, so as that the same two persons should not be
coupled together two successive days; nor should
it be known before hand what two persons are to
be together. To prevent this, the names should
be drawn out every day by lot. By this means,
supposing an offender had succeeded so far in a
project of escape or mischief, as to engage some
one of his comrades to join with him, he could
not, for a long time afterwards, unless by a very
extraordinary turn of chance, resume the con-
versation without the privity of two others, whose
dispositions could not be known before-hand. If
the expedient of a garden were to be employed,
such an arrangement would have a farther good
effect, in rendering it more difficult for them to
wander out of bounds, and do mischief to the
cultivated part of it.

The interruptions of bad weather, and the
shortness of the day, at any other time than the
heighth of summer, would still leave a consider-
able part of their time, which could not be filled

E 4   up

up in this manner : either, therefore, they muft be permitted to employ themfelves in fome other manner, or they muft be compelled to abfolute inaction. They cannot, as other perfons of the working clafs do, employ themfelves on thofe days in vifiting their friends.

They may employ themfelves, it is true, in reading the Bible, or other books of piety ; but there will be a great many who cannot read ; and of thofe who can, many will have fo little inclination, that on pretence of reading, they will do nothing.

It is to little purpofe to iffue directions which, in the nature of them, furnifh no evidence of their having been complied with. The not attending to this, is a common ftumbling-block to fuperficial reformers. The evidence of a man's having complied with a direction to work, is the work he has done : this may be judged of at a glance ; but what is the evidence of a man's having employed himfelf in reading ? His giving a good account of what he has read ? Unqueftionably : but fuch an one as it would be to little purpofe to think of exacting : for, though his attention has been diligent, his memory may be weak. Befides, who is to judge ? who could find time enough to catechize fuch a multitude ? It would require no fmall number of fchoolmafters to turn fuch an eftablifhment into a fchool.

Upon the whole, I can fee no better expedient at prefent than that of permitting them (not *obliging* them, but *permitting* them) to betake them-

felves

felves to fome eafy fedentary employment; fuch as knitting, fpinning, or weaving, that might afford them a fmall profit. This profit, if made their own, would make the employment plea-fant to them. Devotion, it is true, is better on fuch a day than induftry; but induftry is better on every day than total idlenefs; that is, than defpondency or mifchief. The neceffity in this cafe feems at leaft as ftrong as that which has in-duced the legiflature to permit the practice of cer-tain trades on the day in queftion, and which is univerfally underftood to authorize perfons of all defcriptions to purfue moft of their houfehold oc-cupations. It were hard if an inftitution, con-feffedly no original part of the religion we profefs, but only adopted into it by early practice, and in later times fanctioned by human authority, muft, at all events, be permitted to oppofe the main ends of religion, innocence and peace.

I fpeak all along under correction; and what I propofe is only upon the fuppofition, that no other means can be found of filling up their time in a manner more fuitable to the day.

With regard to the making the windows not lefs than fix feet above the floor, this regulation is alfo recommended by Mr. Howard *. His defign in it I cannot find he has any where mentioned. I fuppofe it to be to prevent the convicts from looking out. The profpects or moving fcenes, whatever they might be, which the windows, if lower, might open to their view, might ferve to diftract their attention from their work. This privation,

* P.

privation may be confidered in the light of an independent punifhment, as well as in that of a means of enfuring their fubjection to the other.

Befides this, Mr. Howard is ftrenuous againft glafs windows; he would have nothing but open grating. In this cafe, the height of the windows would be a means, in fome meafure, of fheltering the inhabitants from the wind, though, on the other hand, it would expofe them more to rain. I know not, however, that he has been any where explicit in giving his reafons for reprobating thefe conveniencies.

One reafon may be, the enfuring a continual fupply of frefh air; but this does not feem conclufive. In apartments, indeed, fo crowded and ill-contrived as many of thofe he had occafion to vifit, the windows being glazed, might, by accident, be attended with bad effects; for, I think, he complains in many places, of the clofenefs of fuch rooms, owing, as it feems, either to the windows not being made to open, or to the inattention or ignorance of the gaoler or prifoners in not opening them. But under the excellent regulations provided for thefe houfes, the apartments never will be crowded; they will not be crowded more than thofe of a private houfe; and in a private houfe it never furely was underftood to be neceffary, or even of ufe to health, that there fhould be nothing but grates for windows. If the convicts were to eat in a common room, the fetting open the doors and windows for an hour and a half (which is the time allotted them for meals) would be quite fufficient for the purpofe of ventilation.

Another

Another reafon for having nothing but grating, may be the contributing to give a gloomy and diftrefsful appearance to the outfide of the prifon. This reafon, as far as it applies, feems to be a very good one. But it applies only to the front of the houfe; for this is all that need, or indeed, that ought, to be expofed to the eyes of paffengers. The apartments thus expofed, might be deftined for thofe whofe labour was the hardeft, and whofe treatment, upon the whole, was defigned to be the fevereft; or the whole or a great part might be taken up with common working rooms not made ufe of for lodging rooms.

Section XL. regulates the articles of diet and apparel. For food the convicts are to have

1. Bread, and any coarfe meat, " or " other inferior food."

2. For drink, water or fmall beer.

3. The apparel is to be coarfe and uniform, with certain obvious marks or badges on it. The declared purpofes of thefe marks are, 1ft to humiliate the wearer, 2dly to prevent efcapes.

4. The articles under the above heads are to be ordered in fuch manner as the " Com- " mittee fhall from time to time appoint."

5. No offender is to be permitted to have

any

any other food, " drink, or cloathing, than
" fuch as fhall be fo appointed. '

Perfons wilfully furnifhing him with any
articles of the above kind, other than what
fhall have been fo appointed, are to forfeit
not more than 10*l.* nor lefs than 40*s.*

OBSERVATIONS.

The expedient of marking the apparel is well-
imagined, and quadrates with the practice of feveral foreign countries *. It is defigned, we fee,
to anfwer two purpofes: 1ft, that of a feparate
punifhment, by holding up the wearer in an igno-
minious light: 2dly, that of fafe cuftody, to en-
fure the continuance of the whole punifhment together. The firft of thefe purpofes it may be made
to anfwer as completely as any other that can be
propofed: with refpect to the latter, it will readily
be acknowledged not to be perfectly efficacious.

Marks employed for this purpofe, may be either
temporary or *perpetual.* Againft perpetual marks
in every cafe then, except where the confinement
is meant to be perpetual, there is this conclufive
objection, that they protract a great part of the
punifhment beyond the time that was meant to
be prefcribed to it. Temporary marks may either
be *extraneous* or *inherent.* The marks here propofed are evidently of the former kind. Thefe,
fo long as they continue, are very efficacious

---

* See Howard on Prifons.

means

means of detection, and may be made more palpable than any that are inherent. They serve very well, therefore, as obstacles to an escape during the first moments : in short, until such time as the fugitive can by force or favour procure fresh apparel. But if he is once housed among his friends or confederates, the use of them is at an end. If his person be not known, he may go about boldly like another man.

Inherent marks seem never hitherto to have been thought of. These may be produced by either *mechanical* means or *chymical*.

Instances of *mechanical* means are the partial shaving of the head, or of the beard, or the chin, or mouth ; or the shaving of one eye-brow. But the mark made by the partial shaving of a part of the face, of which the whole is usually kept shaved, is as soon got rid of as any mark that is but extraneous : besides that, it is inapplicable to boys and women. The mark made by the shaving of one eye-brow seems to promise better ; but it is not free from all objections. In the first place it is not absolutely a sure one. Some persons have naturally so little hair on their eye-brows, that, if the whole of it were taken off from both, it might not be missed : and artificial eye-brows are said to have been made of mouse-skin, or in other ways, and that so natural, as not to be detected without previous suspicion. In the next place, there is some danger that a mark continually renewed, as this must be, by repeated shavings, would be in some degree perpetual. If the same eye-brow were to be constantly subjected to the operation, the hair might

be

be so thickened as to appear different from the other eye-brow. If sometimes one eye-brow and sometimes the other were to be shaved, there must frequently be times when the growth of them will be alike, and the distinction no longer apparent. As far then as it goes, the best expedient seems to be the keeping them constantly both shaved.

Instances of *chymical* means of producing marks are washes applied to the forehead, or to one or both cheeks, or, in short, to the whole face, so as to discolour it. Chymistry furnishes many washes of this sort. Of several of these I have often undesignedly made trial upon myself. Various metallic solutions produce this effect in a state so diluted as prevents any objection on the score of expence *. The stain lasts without any fresh application, as long as the *stratum* of skin which it pervades; that is, to the best of my recollection, about a week. No other washes have ever yet been found to discharge it.

Marks of this kind, we see, cannot be put off like those of the former; nor, if made as extensive as they may be, can they be concealed without such a covering as would be almost equally characteristic with the mark itself. When the term of punishment was so near being expired, that it

* Solution of gold in *aqua regia* produces a purplish colour, solution of silver in *aqua fortis*, and solution of mercury in the same acid, a black. Solution of silver is the operative ingredient in several of the fluids that are advertised to dye the hair.

could

could manifeftly not be worth while to run the rifk of an efcape, they might be difufed. For greater fecurity, they might be fo fhaped, perhaps, as to exprefs the furname of the offender, the firft letter of his Chriftian name, and the name of the place in which the labour-houfe he belonged to was fituated. Sect XL. p. 28.

One great advantage of thefe permanent marks with refpect to the offender, is, that they would render the ufe of *chains* lefs neceffary. The convicts upon the *Thames*, in confequence of repeated efcapes, are made to work conftantly in fetters.

By Section XLI. officers and fervants belonging to the houfe are fpecially reftrained from contravening the regulations eftablifhed in the preceding Section. Upon any fuch delinquency the offender is to be fufpended by the governor forthwith: the governor is to report him to the vifitors, and the vifitors to the Committee at their next meeting. The Committee is to enquire upon oath, and, if found guilty, to punifh him by Sect. XLI. p. 29. Penalties on officers infringing the above regulations.

1. Forfeiture of his place;

2. Or fine, not more than ten pounds:

3. Or imprifonment, for not more than fix months.

4. Or any number of fuch punifhments in conjunction.

An

An exception is made with regard to any diet or liquors ordered, in cafe of illnefs, by the furgeon or apothecary.

OBSERVATIONS.

The fine in this and the preceding feƈtion is not liable to the objeƈtion made to the like provifion in feƈtion 29. The profit of the offence can never, in any fhape, come nearly equal to the greateft *quantum* of the fine. Let the offences in the two cafes be compared, it will be feen how much greater the temptation is in the latter than in the former.

The regulations in this and the preceding feƈtion, about not punifhing the conviƈts with any extra articles of confumption, might need to be a little altered, if what I have ventured to propofe concerning the allowing them a part of their earnings * were to be adopted. Thefe earnings muft either be hoarded up for them, to be given them at their difcharge, or allowed them to be fpent. In the firft cafe, the danger is, left an advantage fo diftant, fhould not, in their imprudent minds, have influence enough to operate as an inducement. " I may be dead before then," a man may fay, " and what ufe will all the money " be of to me ? befides, if I am alive, how can " I be fure that I fhall get it ? What need have I " then to punifh myfelf with working more than

* See Obfervations to Seƈt. XXIII.

" I am

" I am obliged to do ?"—I fhould not, therefore, expect any very general or confiderable good effect from fuch an allowance, without the liberty of fpending it, or at leaft a part of it, in prefent. The bufinefs then would be, to determine the articles in which they might be allowed to fpend it. Even drink, fo it be not any of thofe drinks that are known commonly by the name of fpiri-tuous liquors, need not be abfolutely excluded : but, for very good reafons, which are ftrongly infifted on by Mr. Howard †, no profit upon the drink fhould be allowed to the governor, or any perfons under him; or elfe (what would come nearly to the fame thing) if there were a profit allowed upon that article, it fhould not be greater, nor indeed fo great, as the profit to be allowed upon the other articles among which they were to be permitted to take their choice. The fmallnefs of their fund would probably of itfelf be fufficient to limit their confumption within the bounds of fobriety. If not, the quantity of drink of each fort, which any one man fhould be al-lowed to purchafe, might be exprefsly limited. The circumftances of their being fo much apart from one another, and fo much under the eye of their infpectors, would obviate the difficulty there would be otherwife in carrying fuch a limitation into effect.

---

† P. 49.

F   Section

Se&t.
XLII.
p. 29.

Section XLII. makes provision for the equipment of the offender upon his discharge. Upon his commitment, the cloaths he brings with him are to be cleaned, ticketed, and laid up. Upon his discharge they are to be delivered back to him, together with such additional cloathing as the visitors shall think proper. A sum of money is also to be allowed him for his immediate subsistence, to the amount of not more than Five Pounds, nor less than Forty Shillings. And if he has behaved himself well during his confinement, the visitors are to give him a certificate to that effect under their hands.

OBSERVATIONS.

There is something singularly characteristic in the foresight and humanity displayed in this provision. It is copied from the experimental act of 1776. After a long seclusion, the convict is once more turned adrift into society. His former connections are by this time, perhaps, dissolved; by death, by change of abode, or by estrangement: at any rate, he is probably at a distance from them. His known delinquency and his punishment, though, after such a course of discipline, it is to be hoped it will not operate upon *all* persons so as to prevent their employing him, may, however, operate upon *many*. Mean time, if he be

3

totally

totally unprovided, he muſt either ſink at once into the idleneſs and miſery of a poor-houſe, or beg, or ſtarve, or betake himſelf to courſes ſimilar to thoſe which brought him to the place of puniſhment he is juſt freed from. The expedient, therefore, of giving him a temporary ſupply, is an highly proper one; though not ſo obvious as for the credit of human ſagacity and compaſſion it were to be wiſhed it were.

But ſuppoſing an offender's behaviour to have been ſuch as renders it improper for the Viſitors to give him the certificate here mentioned. What is to become of him then? Were no certificate to be given in any caſe, ſome perſons might, perhaps, be induced to run the hazard of employing a convict, to whom it would not have been proper to have granted one. But when it is known that a certificate of good behaviour is granted to the generality of the convicts, the denial of ſuch a certificate to any one amounts in fact to a certificate of the contrary. In ſuch a caſe, it is not very probable that he will find employment any where. The ſupply provided for him, liberal as it is, can *reprieve* him only, not *ſave* him, from the above-mentioned dilemma.

In ſuch a caſe, I ſee but two courſes that can be taken. One is, to impower the Committee to continue him in his confinement, till his behaviour ſhall have entitled him to his certificate: the other is to enliſt him by compulſion in the land or ſea ſervice. How far it would be conſiſtent with the honour of either of theſe ſervices to

F 2 admit

admit a man with fuch a ftamp of uncancelled ignominy upon him, is more than I can take upon me to determine. At any rate, it feems hardly proper to let him rank upon a par with honeft men. In the fea fervice, provifions being found him, his pay might very well bear to be reduced below the common level : in the land fervice, provifions not being allowed, the fubfiftance is too bare to admit of the leaft reduction.

It is to be hoped, indeed, that after fo ftrict and well-regulated a courfe of difcipline as that prefcribed by the bill, there will be very few convicts to whom it will be neceffary to deny the certificate in queftion ; but it is fit that every cafe that can happen, fhould be provided for.

Sect.
XLIII.
p. 30.
Convicts
to be di-
vided into
claffes. Section XLIII. provides that the offenders fhall be divided into three claffes ; in each of which every offender is to ranked, during an equal part of his time : and as he advances from a prior to a fubfequent one, his confinement and labour are to be gradually lefs and lefs fevere. The different gradations of feverity are to be fettled from time to time by regulations to be made by the Committee, fo as not to clafh with the provifions of this Bill.

OBSERVATIONS.

This divifion of the convicts into claffes will be exam'ned, when we come to confider the ufes that are made of it.

Section

Section XLIV. regulates the furniture and police of the lodging-rooms.

Sect.
XLIV.
p. 30.
Furniture
and po
lice of the
*Lodging-
rooms.*

1. Every lodging-room is to be " pro-
" vided with matting for lying upon, a
" coverlid, and two or more coarfe blan-
" kets."

2. " Alfo with proper tools or inftruments
" for their employment."

3. No perfon (except as herein is excepted) is to " be permitted to go at any
" time into thefe rooms, or to fee or con-
" verfe with the offenders."

4. Perfons excepted are, 1. The officers
and fervants of the houfe: 2. Any perfon
who has an order from any member of the
Committee.

5. At night, as foon as the time of work
is over, a bell is to be rung, the doors of
the rooms locked, and the lights in them
put out: and from that time, till the hour
of work comes round again, a watchman is
to patrole over every part of the houfe every
half hour at leaft.

OBSERVATIONS.

Under the article of bedding, I fee no mention
made of *fheets*. Was this omiffion undefigned, or
was it meant that they fhould have none ? or
would not the ufe of linen, if not abfolutely ne-

F 3   ceffary,

ceffary, at leaft be conducive however to the pre-
fervation of their health ? Mr. Hume, I think, in
his hiftory, Mr. Barrington †, and, I believe, medical writers, have mentioned the ufe of linen as
being a principal caufe why the leprofy, which
was once fo common in this country, is now fo
rare.

I fee no mention neither of a *bed-ftead.* Mr.
Howard in general terms recommends bed-fteads
for health and cleanlinefs *. A bed-ftead, however cold the materials (fuppofe iron) will be
warmer than the ftone or brick floor, with only
matting to cover it ; for the furface of the iron in
the bedftead being much lefs than that of the covered
part of the floor, the natural warmth of the body,
accumulated on the bedding, will be conducted
away much lefs readily by the former than by the
latter. At any rate, the elevation given by a bed-
ftead will fave the bedding from being trampled
on and covered with duft and dirt. It will alfo
give accefs for the air to ventilate the under part
of it.

Bed-fteads are actually allowed to felons in
many gaols ‡.

I fee no provifion made here for *firing :* yet
fome provifion of this fort feems abfolutely necef-
ary, at leaft, in extreme cold weather, for thofe

---

† Obfervations on the Statutes, Title *Confuetudines
et Affifa Foreftæ,* p. 193. 3d edit.

* P. 71. 264.

‡ Howard, 96, 264, 292, 404, 407, 443, 454.

whofe

whofe employments are chiefly of the fedentary kind, and for all of them at times, when no work is done, as on Sundays. For this purpofe, it is by no means neceffary, nor even advifeable, that there fhould be a fire to every room, nor between every two rooms, nor indeed that there fhould be in any of the rooms any fire-places at all. The moft oeconomical way as yet in ufe, of generating and applying heat for this purpofe, feems to be that which is practifed in *hot-houfes*, by means of flues or lateral chimnies, in which the fmoke depofits its heat in its paffage to the atmo-fphere. The fire employed in heating the bread-oven, might, perhaps, be occafionally made ufe-ful in this way. I have heard it fuggefted, that the fteam of boiling water might perhaps be ap-plied to the purpofe of heating rooms, in a method that might be more oeconomical than that of heat-ing them by fmoke. If this expedient were em-ployed, the coppers in which the victuals were boiled, might perhaps be adapted to this pur-pofe *.

The provifion for excluding promifcuous vifi-tants feems highly eligible. In a nation, how-ever, fo jealous of every thing that favours of fecrecy in the exercife of coercive power, even over the moft obnoxious of its members, it required no mean degree of intrepidity to propofe it. I had, in truth, but little hope of feeing it pro-

---

* Mr. Howard found ftoves, and a regular provifion for firing, in feveral foreign prifons. See How. 109, 114, 137.

pofed,

poſed, much leſs adopted and acquieſced in, as it already is in the inſtance of the Thames convicts. An acquieſcence ſo complete and general as this has been found to be, argues a greater fund of ſolid ſenſe, and leſs ſenſibility to inflammatory ideas, than perhaps, before the experiment was made, could reaſonably have been hoped for. This, together with many other examples to the like effect, may ſerve to ſilence at leaſt, if not to remove, any objections that may be entertained againſt a meaſure acknowledged to be beneficial in itſelf, on the ſcore of its being obnoxious to popular ſentiment, unwarranted by the dictates of utility.

The eſtabliſhment of Viſitors, who are frequently to be changed, and the admiſſion of occaſional viſitants by order from any member of the Committees, are expedients that ſeem amply ſufficient for obviating any real danger of abuſive ſeverity. It is ſurely a notion too wild to be ſeriouſly entertained, by any one who will give himſelf leiſure to reflect, that the whole body of country magiſtrates, and the whole circle of their acquaintance, are likely to be tainted with the principles of ariſtocratic tyranny. Suppoſing this, againſt all probability, to be the caſe, and that any one habit of undue ſeverity were eſtabliſhed, any one falſe brother would be ſufficient to betray the ſecrets of the confederacy, and expoſe it to the reſentment of the public.

At the ſame time, it is highly expedient to give as little admittance as poſſible to perſons of ſuch ranks in life as are moſt obnoxious to the pu

nifhment inflicted in thefe houfes. The circumftances of fecrecy and feclufion give an air of
myftery to the fcene, which contributes greatly to
enhance the terrors it is intended to imprefs. True
it is, that the convicts, as they come to be dif-
charged, and to mix again with fociety, will cir-
culate, among perfons of the fame ranks in life,
fuch accounts of what they have feen and felt,
as it may be thought will be fufficient to correct any inaccuracies in the notions that may
have been fuggefted by imagination ; this however,
I take it, will not be altogether the cafe. Experience and ocular obfervation might indeed, in
time, diffipate the illufion, and bring down the
apparent horrors of the fcene to a level with the
real fuffering ; but in the fufceptible minds of
the giddy multitude, it is not mere report alone
that can obliterate the influence of firft impref-
fions.

Section XLV. makes provifion for com-
municating to thefe focieties the benefits
of religion.

   1. On all Sundays, as alfo on Chriftmas-
day, and Good-Friday, there is to be morning and evening fervice, with a fermon
after each : at which fervices all the convicts
(unlefs difabled by illnefs) are to be prefent.

   2. The two fexes are to be kept at a
diftance

Sect. XLIV. p. 30.

Sect. XLV. p. 31. Provifion for *religious* du-ties.

diſtance from, and, by means of partitions, out of ſight of, one another.

3. Of the officers and ſervants, ſuch as can be ſpared from their employments, are likewiſe (unleſs prevented by illneſs) to be preſent.

4. The chaplain is required to viſit, at their requeſt, and empowered to viſit at his own diſcretion, any of the offenders, ſick or in health, who may ſtand in need of his ſpiritual aſſiſtance: ſo that his viſits interfere not with their ſtated labours.

OBSERVATIONS.

It were to be wiſhed on this occaſion, if it could be done without inconvenience, that ſuch of the convicts as may happen to be of a religion different from the eſtabliſhed, might have the benefit of ſpiritual conſolation in their own way. It is no anſwer, to ſay with a ſneer, that the inhabitants of theſe houſes are in little likelihood of being incumbered with religious ſcruples; for a total indifference to religion is by no means a neceſſary accompanyment to an occaſional deviation from the dictates of morality: on the contrary, it is no uncommon thing to obſerve in the ſame perſon, a great inattention to the eſſentials of morality, joined to an anxious attention to the ineſſentials and externals of religion. This point, however, could not be compaſſed without ſome difficulty. It would be endleſs to ſet up as many chapels as
there

Sect.
XLV.
p. 51.

there may chance to be sects in this community.
At any rate, it is not the belonging or professing
to belong to any other sect, that should be allowed to excuse a man from attending the stated
service; for, if this were the case, persons who
cared nothing about religion, would be apt to pro-
fess themselves of some dissenting sect, that, in-
stead of going to chapel, they might spend the
time in idleness. The being obliged to give such
attendance, would be no hardship to any, even in a
religious view; for I do not believe there is at this
time of day any sect which holds it sinful merely
to be present at divine service performed according to the rites of the church of England *. I
suppose there are few, indeed, but would even
think it better to attend that service than none
at all.

Jews and *Catholics* would be the worst off: Jews,
with their continual domestic ceremonies, and
Catholics with their numerous sacraments. Catholics † seem, at first sight, to be without hope
of remedy: a door, however, though but a narrow
one, is opened for their relief, by the general
power vested in the members of the Committees
to give orders of admission. As to *Jews*, I must

---

* In the prisons at Paris however Protestants are
excused from hearing mass. See Howard, 81.

† By Stat. 27 Eliz. c 2. for a popish priest or other
ecclesiastical person to be in any part of the realm is
treason: and for any one wittingly and willingly to receive, relieve, or comfort him is a capital felony.

confess,

confefs, I can fee no feafible way of making, in each labour-houfe, the provifions requifite for fatisfying all their various fcruples. As it happens, there feems reafon (I do not know whether to fay to hope, but at any rate) to believe, that of fuch of them as are likely to become inhabitants of thefe houfes there are not many on whom thefe fcruples would fit heavy. The only expedient I can think of for the indulgence of thefe people is, to have one labour-houfe for all the convicts of this perfuafion throughout the kingdom. In fuch cafe, it would be but reafonable that the whole community of Jews fhould be at the expence of this eftablifhment, including the charges of conveyance. They might then have their own *Rabbies,* and their own cooks and butchers.

The provifion for the concealment of the fexes from each other, has been exemplified by the practice in the *Magdalen* and other chapels.

In fome of the larger houfes, confidering the number of perfons, either fick or in health, who might be difpofed to receive the affiftance of a minifter, or to whom a zealous minifter might be difpofed to give it, efpecially if thefe additions were to be made to the fervice that are propofed under fection 39, a fingle chaplain might hardly be fufficient to go through all the duty. In fuch cafe, the contributions that might be required of occafional vifitors at chapel, who are likely to become numerous, might probably provide for another chaplain.

Section

Section 58, which relates to convicts working upon rivers, provides for the burial of such as die under confinement. I fee no fuch provifion relative to fuch as may die in the labour-houfes. Would it not be proper to annex to each houfe a piece of ground to be confecrated for that purpofe ?

Section XLVI. makes provifion for the article of health.

1. There are to be two or more yards, in which the offenders are to be permitted to take the air by turns, as their health may require: in thefe yards, if proper employment can be found, they are alfo to be permitted to work, inftead of working in the houfe.

2. Any offender appearing to be fick, is, upon report made by the furgeon or apothecary that his ficknefs is real, to be ordered by the governor to the infirmary, if his ficknefs be of a nature to require it, and entered in a book upon the fick lift : and upon the furgeon or apothecary's report of his being recovered and fit to work, he is to be brought back to his lodging-room and put to work again, as far as is confiftent with his health.

Sect. XLV. p. 31.

Sect. XLVI. p. 31. —health.

O B-

OBSERVATIONS.

The number of yards is required, we fee, to be two at leaft: the intention is manifeft enough, though it is not mentioned: it is, that the two fexes may, in conformity to the plan of feparation marked out in fections 38 and 41, have each a yard to themfelves.

As to the purpofe of airing, the beft place of all is the top of the houfe. The air on the top of the houfe is likely to be purer than the air in any yards can be, furrounded as fuch yards muft be by a high wall: 1ft, fuch a fituation would be higher than the damp or the noxious effluvia would afcend, were the air to remain unchanged: 2dly, befides this, the air, on account of the opennefs of the fituation, would, in fact, be continually renewing *. For this purpofe, it would be ne-ceffary the roof of the houfe fhould be flat, and covered with lead. The infirmary might be fituated in the higheft ftory; fo that from thence to the leads would be but a few fteps. It is doubtlefs for thefe or fimilar reafons, that a fituation thus elevated is very generally chofen for the infirmary in foreign prifons †. In order that thofe whofe health might require it, might enjoy the benefits of air and exercife in fome degree, even in rainy weather, it would be of great ufe if the building, or a great part of it, were raifed upon arcades. This Mr. Howard recommends ftrong-

---

* Howard, 82, 91.   † Ibid. 82, 91, 96.

ly

ly for fo much of it as is occupied by lodging-rooms, on the fcore of fecurity.

The expence, indeed, of building upon arches, and of leading, would be very confiderable ; but the plan feems to be not to fpare expence. The Conciergerie at Paris *, the Dol-huys at Amfter-dam †, the Maifon de force at Ghent ‡, are raifed upon arcades ‖ : in the Baftile at Paris, the roof is flat and leaded. I muft confefs, I fee not why England fhould be lefs able to bear fuch an expence than France, Holland, or Auftrian Flanders.

Section XLVII. regulates the appointment, powers, and falaries of the Vifitors.

1. Each Committee is to appoint two vifitors, " Juftices of the Peace, or other fubftantial houfholders," who are to be refident in the diftrict.

2. Of thefe vifitors, one is to be changed every year: no one is to continue for more than two fucceffive years; but any one, after an interval of two years, may be again appointed.

3. The Vifitors are to attend at leaft once in every fortnight.

Sect. XLVI, P. 31.

Sect. XLVII. P. 32. Vifitors —their appointment, powers, and emoluments.

---

* Howard, 82.   † Ibid. 128.
‡ Ibid. 140.   ‖ Ibid. 82.

4. At

4. At each attendance they are to go through the following heads of duty:

1. To examine the state of the " house" [buildings].

2. To see every convict.

3. To inspect the accounts of the governor and store-keepers.

4. To hear any complaints concerning the behaviour of the officers and servants.

5. Or of the convicts.

6. And in general to examine into the conduct and management of the house.

5. For these purposes every visitor is impowered to examine any persons upon oath.

6. They are likewise empowered to apply punishments or rewards as under-mentioned.

7. They are from time to time to make their reports to the Judges *, as before, or to the Committee of the district.

8. They are to have a gratuity, if they think proper to demand it, for each attendance, to be settled by the Committee, and approved of by the Judges.

---

* See Sect. 11, 21, 24, 26, 30.

O B-

OBSERVATIONS.

The rotation eſtabliſhed among theſe officers is grounded upon approved principles, that are exemplified in many other inſtances. If the ſame two Viſitors were to be continued for life, the degree of diſcipline kept up in the houſe might come to depend more upon the notions and temper of thoſe two perſons, than upon ſettled rules. Having no emulation to animate them, they might grow torpid and indifferent: they might contraƈt too cloſe an intimacy with the governor and other officers, ſo as to be diſpoſed to connive at their negligence or peculation: they might make what is called a *job* of their offices, looking upon the emoluments of it as an eſtabliſhment for life. On the other hand, were both Viſitors to go out at once, the freſh comers would for a time be new and awkward in their office; and the fund of experience collected at each period, would be diſſipated by every freſh appointment. But upon this plan, that fund is continually accummulating, and is tranſmitted entire through every ſucceſſion. At the ſame time, by admitting the re-election of a Viſitor after a certain interval, room is left for accepting the ſervices of ſuch gentlemen as in point of inclination and ability may ſhew themſelves moſt competent to the office.

Section XLVIII. gives power to the Viſitors to ſuſpend any officer or ſervant, except

Seƈt. XLVII. P. 32.

Seƈt. XLVIII. P. 33.
Power to

G

fufpend
officers.

cept the Governor, in cafe of " corruption,
" or other grofs mifbehaviour."

Sect.
XLIX.
P. 33.
*Tafk-maf-
ters*, their
duty.

Section XLIX. appoints the duty of the
Tafk-mafter.

1. He is conftantly to fuperintend the
works carried on by the convicts.

2. He is to " take an account of every
" neglect of work or other mifbehaviour.

3. Alfo of any inftance of extraordinary
diligence or good behaviour.

4. He is to make his reports from time
to time to the Governor, who is to caufe
them to be entered in a book to be kept for
that purpofe.

Sect. L.
P. 33.
Powers of
the Go-
vernor in
punifhing
offences
commit-
ted in the
houfe.

Section L. defines the powers of the Governor in punifhing offences committed in
the houfe.   Thefe are enumerated under the
following heads :

1. Difobedience of the " orders of-
" the houfe."

2. Idlenefs, negligence, or wilful mif-
management of work.

3. Affaults not attended with any
dangerous wound or bruife by one convict upon another.

4. Indecent behaviour.

5. Profane curfing and fwearing.

6. Ab-

6. Abfence from chapel.

7. Irreverent behaviour at chapel.

2. For any of the above offences the governor may punifh by clofe confinement in a " cell or dungeon," for any term not exceeding three days, and keeping the offender upon bread and water only.

3. Touching any of the above offences, the governor may examine " *any*" perfons upon oath.

Sect. LI.
P. 34.
—of Vifi-
'tors and
Commit-
tees.

Section LI. impowers the Vifitors and the Committee to punifh certain other inftances of bad behaviour in a feverer manner.

1. To the Vifitors power is given to punifh, in any convict, the following additional offences:

1. Abfolute refufal to perform his work.

2. Wilful abufe of the materials.

3. Attemps to efcape.

4. Affaults on any perfon at large, who happens to be prefent.

5. Affaults on any officer or fervant of the houfe.

2. They are empowered alfo to punifh any affaults by one convict upon another, that

may

may happen not to have been punifhed by the Governor.

3. Alfo any of the offences which the Governor is authorized to punifh in the cafe where, by reafon of the enormity or re-petition of the offence, the punifhment which the Governor is empowered to inflict of his own authority, is thought by him not to be fufficient.

4. For any of the above offences the vi-fitors may punifh by either

1. Moderate whipping.

2. Confinement upon bread and water in a dungeon, for any time not exceed-ing ten days.

3. Or both the above punifhments in conjunction.

5. Concerning the above offences they are empowered to examine upon oath, with an injunction that it be in the prefence of the of-fender.

6. In the cafes No. 2. and 3. " *the go-* " *vernor may, and he is hereby required to,* " *order fuch offender to the cells or dungeons,—* " *and is immediately,*" or at the next coming of the Vifitors, to " *report fuch offence to fuch* " *Vifitors ; who are hereby empowered and re-* " *quired to enquire and determine concerning* " *the fame.*"

7. In

7. In cafe of any offence which the Vifitors fhall deem worthy of a greater pu-nifhment than they are authorized to inflict, they fhall report the offence, with the nature and circumftances of it, and the name of the offender, to the next meeting of the Com-mittee.

8. To the Committee power is given to punifh offences thus reported to them, by either

    1. Moderate whipping.

    2. Confinement upon bread and water in a dungeon.

    3. Turning down from a higher clafs to a lower.

    4. All or any of the above punifh-ments in conjunction.

9. " *In cafe of removal into a prior clafs,* " *the offender fhall, from the time of making* " *fuch order of removal, go through fuch prior* " *clafs, and alfo the fubfequent clafs or claffes,* " *in the fame manner, and for the fame time as* " *under his or her original commitment.*"

Section LII. is the converfe of the Section laft preceding : it opens a door to pardon upon the ground of extraordinary *good* be-haviour.

1. If

1. If in any convict committed by Juftices in Seffions, the Vifitors " fhall at any time " obferve, or be fatisfactorily informed of, " any extraordinary diligence or merit," and make report accordingly, " the faid Juftices" [fhall] " may, if they think proper, advance him into a higher clafs."

2. When any convict has been promoted as above, the time of his confinement is to " be computed as if he or fhe had regularly " paffed through the prior clafs or claffes."

3. With regard to any convicts committed by the Judges *, whether originally, or upon a pardon granted upon that condition, for a certain term, the Judges are, upon a like report, to have like power to alter and fhorten his confinement.

4. Convicts, committed for life, may, upon being reported to the Judges as aforefaid, be by them reported to his Majefty for mercy.

OBSERVATIONS.

This and the two laft preceding fections bearing a clofe relation to one another, I fhall confider them together. As to the laft of the two

---

* At the Old Bailey, or on the Circuits.

para-

paragraphs I have printed in Italics I muſt confeſs I am not altogether certain about the ſenſe of it. My doubt is, whether a convict, upon his degradation into a lower claſs, is to be puniſhed with reſpect to the ſeverity of his treatment only, or, beſides that, with reſpect to the duration of his confinement. I am inclined to imagine, both ways ; but this conſtruction ſeems not to be abſolutely a neceſſary one.

A convict, ſuppoſe, has been committed for three years. He has ſerved the firſt year of his time, and half his ſecond. Of courſe, he has been half a year entered in the ſecond claſs. He now commits an offence which the Committee think proper to. puniſh with degradation : he is turned down into the firſt claſs. What now is to become of him ? Is he to ſtay two years and a half longer, to wit, one half year more in the firſt claſs, and a year in each of the other claſſes, or only one year and a half, that is, half a year in each of the three claſſes ? In the firſt caſe, it ſeems hardly proper to ſay, that he has gone through " ſuch prior " claſs, and alſo the ſubſequent claſſes in the " ſame manner, and for the *ſame time*, as under " his original commitment;" for it ſeems that he has gone through ſuch prior claſs, and alſo the ſubſequent claſſes (in the ſame manner, perhaps, but) for a *longer* time than he was to have had to go through them in under his original commitment Had there, however, been no diſtinction in the treatment to be given to the reſpective claſſes, it muſt have been underſtood in this ſenſe, as pro-

longing

longing the total time; for the provifion would
have had nothing but the circumftance of time to
operate upon.

Another doubt I have refpecting the claufe in
fection 50, which limits the time for which a governor is impowered to keep a convict in a
dungeon upon bread and water to *three* days.
This paffage I know not very well how to recon-
cile to a claufe in fection 51. In this latter fection, in cafe of an offence which, in the opinion
of the governor, deferves a greater punifhment
than what he is himfelf authorized to inflict, he is
directed to report it to the Vifitors, who, in fuch
cafe, are authorized to order the offender to confinement in a dungeon, there to be kept on bread
and water, if that be the mode of punifhment they
think proper to adopt, for ten days. Thus far,
then, their power extends; to the confining a
man for ten days. To the governor, in the laft
preceding fection, it was not thought proper to
give fo great a power: his power was to extend
no farther than to the confining a man for three
days; yet in this fame fection, in the cafe above
mentioned, where, by the fuppofition he cannot
punifh by confinement for more than *three* days,
the Governor is impowered and "required" to
order the convict to the dungeon, and "imme-
"diately, or the next time the Vifitors fhall
"come," report the offence to them, for them
to punifh it. Now, for what time the convict
committed in this manner to a dungeon is to remain there, is not exprefsly faid: as no time is

mentioned

mentioned for his releafement, it feems impof-
fible to put any other conftruction upon the claufe
than that he is to ftay there till the coming of the
Vifitors. But the Vifitors may not come for a
fortnight *. So long then may a convict remain
in one of thefe dungeons by the authority of a
Governor. The confequence is, 'that indirectly
a power is given to this officer, of inflicting a punifhment more than three times as great as that
which it is thought proper, in direct terms, to
impower him to inflict; and (as far as concerns
this fpecies of punifhment) greater than that which
it has been thought proper, in any terms; to impower the Vifitors to inflict. On this occafion,
no mention, I obferve, is made of dieting upon
bread and water : the Governor is fimply required
to order the offender to one of the dungeons. Is
he then, or is he not in this cafe, authorized to
add that hardfhip to the confinement? Is the dieting in this manner, or is it not, to be regarded
as an article included of courfe in the regimen of
a dungeon ? This power of punifhing an offender
previoufly to trial, is confined, I obferve, to the
Governor : it is not given to the Vifitors.

The provifion for difpofing of the convicts into claffes †, fo as to be liable to be advanced or
to be degraded ‡, feems an excellent expedient for
ftrengthening the influence of the feveral authorities to which it is meant to fubject them. It feems

---

* See Sect. 47.   † See Sect. 43.
‡ See Sect. 51.

extremely

Sect. LII.
P. 35.

extremely well contrived for exciting emulation ; for making a standing and palpable distinction betwixt good and ill behaviour, and for keeping their hopes and fears continually awake. If it should be thought proper to indulge the convicts with a share in the profit of the labour *, this would afford a farther means of adding to the distinction.

Here ends that part of the bill which concerns the establishment of labour-houses. What follows in the seven next sections is confined to the system of labour to be carried on upon rivers. The greater part of them are employed in re-enacting so many corresponding clauses of the present act †. Concerning these, it will not be necessary to be very particular.

Sect. LIII. p. 36. Superintendants, how to employ their convicts.

Section LIII. establishes, in general terms, the authority of the Superintendants above spoken of ‡. It empowers them, upon the delivery of any *male* convict into their custody, to keep him, for the term mentioned in his sentence, to hard labour. This hard labour is to be applied " either to the raising " of sand, soil, and gravel, or in any other

---

* See Observations on Sect. 23.

† The name given to the head person who is to have the charge of the convicts upon this establishment is changed from *Overseer* (the word used in the former act) to *Superintendant.*

‡ See Sect. 32, 33, 34, 36.

                                       " la-

" laborious fervice for the benefit of the
" navigation of the *Thames*, or of fuch
" other navigable rivers, or harbours, as
" aforefaid * :" when on the *Thames*, " then
" at fuch places only, and fubject to fuch
" limitations, as the Trinity-Houfe fhall,
" from time to time, prefcribe."

Sect.
LIII.
p. 36.

OBSERVATIONS.

This, as to the greater part of it, is an exact
tranfcript of the latter part of fection 5. of the
prefent act †.

Section LIV. prohibits Superintendants
from employing their convicts in delivering
ballaft to fhips : it reftricts the application
of the labour to the above-mentioned object
of benefiting the navigation of the rivers or
harbours in queftion : except that it permits
the employing them in making or repairing
embankments or fea-walls.

Sect.
LIV.
p. 36.
—not in
deliver-
ing *ballaft*
to veffels.

OBSERVATIONS.

This fection is an exact tranfcript of fection 6. of
the prefent act, with the addition only of the

---

* See Sect. 32.

† By *the prefent act* I mean all along the Stat. 16
.Geo. 3d. ch. 43. being that which is in force at the
time I write.

above

Sect.
LIV.
P. 36.

above exception. As this new kind of employment was meant to be permitted, the infertion of the above exceptiod for that purpofe, was no more than prudent, at leaft, if not abfolutely neceffary : for the main defign in making of embankments or fea-walls, is to·fave the land from being carried away or overflowed ; and it may be of little or no fervice to the navigation. Mr. Campbell, Superintendant of the Thames convicts, purfuing the fpirit of his inftructions rather than the letter, has already ventured to employ his convicts in fome ufeful works on fhore ; perhaps it might not be amifs to add a retrofpective claufe for his indemnity.

As to the prohibition above mentioned, no reafon for it is given. I imagine the reafon to have been the preventing that intercommunication which in fuch a cafe, would have been neceffary between the convicts and the fhips-crews. It can have nothing to do with any privileges of the Trinity-houfe ; not being confined to the Thames, but extended to all rivers and harbours where convicts fhall be employed.

Sect. LV.
P. 37.
—how to
diet and
cloath
them.

Section LV. provides for the diet and apparel of convicts, under the care of fuperintendants, as Section XL. did for thofe who are to be confined in the Labour-houfes. In point of diet it directs that they be fed with bread, and any coarfe or inferior food, and water or fmall beer, as in Section XL. only
the

the word " *meat* " is dropped here after the word coarfe (whether by accident or defign is more than I can determine). The apparel it leaves altogether to the " difcretion of the " fuperintendants :" it likewife prohibits the fupplying the convicts with any other food, drink, or cloathing, under a penalty of not more than ten pounds, nor lefs than forty fhillings.

OBSERVATIONS.

This fection is the fame as fection 7. of the prefent act ; except with regard to the penalty which, by the prefent act, is not to be more than forty fhillings.

Sect.
LVI.
P. 37.
—and
correct
them.

Section LVI. invefts fuperintendants with the power of correction. A convict refufing to perform his work, or " *guilty of any other* " *mifbehaviour or diforderly conduct,*" may be punifhed by the fuperintendant, by " fuch " whipping, or other moderate punifhment, " as may be inflicted by law on perfons " committed to a houfe of correction for " hard labour."

OBSERVATIONS.

This fection is the fame in every refpect as fection 8. of the prefent act.

Section

Section LVII. provides a supply for convicts of this description, upon their discharge, to the same amount as Section LII. did for the convicts in the Labour-houses. It likewise provides for the discharge of any convict, previous to the expiration of his term, upon a letter written, upon a recommendation from the Judges as in Sect. LX. by a Secretary of State. The sum of money, and the cloathing, it refers, in this case, to the determination of the above Judges.*

OBSERVATIONS.

This section is the same, in every respect, as section 9. of the present act.

Section LVIII. makes provision in the lump for the assistance, medical and religious, to be given to the convicts in question, as likewise for the burial of such as may chance to die, as also for these and all other expences attending the keeping of the convicts under the care of such Superintendants These expences it directs to be annually laid before the House of Commons, and undertakes, that, after deducting the net profits (if any) of the labour, they shall

* See Sect. 11, 21, 24, 26, 30, 47, 52.

be provided for in the next supplies granted by Parliament. The chaplains, surgeons, and apothecaries to be provided, are to be such as " the Superintendant shall find it " expedient, or shall be required" (it does not say by whom) " from time to time to " employ." The convicts are to be " *buried* " in the most commodious parts of the " shores, in or near which they have been " employed," and " according to the form " prescribed by the Liturgy of the Church " of England. The necessary charges of " such funerals, and also of the coroners, " who shall sit on the bodies of such con- " victs, are to be defrayed in the manner above-mentioned.

Sect. LVIII. p. 38.

Section LIX. provides, that such chaplains shall read morning and evening *prayer*, and preach a *sermon* after each, every Sunday, as also on Christmas-day and Good Friday.

Sect. LIX. p. 38. Provision for divine service.

OBSERVATIONS.

These two sections are so many additions to the present act. In this the whole business was referred so entirely to the discretion of the Superintendant, that no express provision was made for either the spiritual or medical assistance, or the burial of the convicts. Neither was any provision made for the

the coroner's fees ; whereby that expence (which
was not altogether a trifling one) falls folely as yet
upon the counties bordering that part of the
Thames they are employed upon ; that is, upon
the counties of *Kent* and *Effex*, one or both of
them. Thefe omiffions are fupplied in the bill
before, as it was highly requifite they fhould be.

In the mean time, they have been voluntarily
fupplied by the attention of Mr. Campbell, the
prefent Superintendant. A furgeon of a battalion
attends the convicts once a day ; and the furgeon
general of the artillery vifits them once a week.
A clergyman fent by the countefs of Hunt-
ingdon, gives them the affiftances belonging to
his profeffion, without any gratuity from Mr.
Campbell, or any expence to the eftablifhment.
Not content with performing the ordinary duty
in the manner provided for in the bill, he is af-
fiduous in giving them the benefit of his inftructions by every means, and at every opportu-
nity in his power. He has diftributed Bibles
among them ; and has endeavoured to direct their
attention to the facred writings, by giving them
rewards for performing little exercifes propofed to
them as tefts of their proficiency.

The loofe and general way in which thefe and
other exigencies are provided for, with refpect to
convicts of the defcription now before us, efpecially when compared with the ftrict and minute
attention paid to the regimen of the labour-houfes,
are ftrong teftimonies of the extraordinary confidence repofed in the prefent Superintendant. I
have

2

have never heard of any fact fo much as furmifed, that afforded the leaft reafon for deeming that confidence mifplaced ; and I have much reafon for entertaining a contrary opinion; yet I fhould be forry to fee the merit of this individual officer made an argument for entailing powers fo unlimited upon what perfon foever may chance at any time hereafter to bear his office. The eftablifhment upon the Thames has been acknowledged to be intended but as a meafure of experiment ; it is to be hoped therefore, that when the effect of the regimen prefcribed for the hard-labour houfes has been approved by experience, it will be extended to the eftablifhments upon rivers. *Jealoufy, not confidence, is the characterifitic of wife laws.*

Section LX. enjoins the Governors and Superintendants to make returns of the ftate of the convicts under their care. Thefe returns are to contain the following particulars :

    1. The name of each convict committed to their cuftody.

    2. His offence.

    3. His fentence.

    4. His ftate of body.

    5. His behaviour while in cuftody.

They are alfo to exhibit the names of all fuch convicts, as, fince the laft return, have paffed out of their cuftody, whether

    1. By death.

H   2. By

2. By efcape.

3. By releafement, whether by order of a Secretary of State or otherwife.

For the purpofe of making thefe returns regular *books* are to be kept by the perfons who are refpectively to make them.

They are to be made by the fuperinten-dant of the Thames convicts to the King's-bench, the firft day of every term: by the governors of Labour-houfes, and the fuper-intendants of any other work, to the Judges, as before *, at each Affize; to the Juftices of the Peace for every county and divifion within the diftrict, at the two Seffions holden next after Eafter and Michaelmas.

They are to be made upon oath, to be adminiftered to them by the refpective courts.

OBSERVATIONS.

The ordering thefe returns is a meafure of excel-lent ufe in furnifhing *data* for the legiflator to go to work upon. They will form all together a kind of *political barometer*, by which the effect of every legiflative operation relative to this fubject, may be indicated and made palpable. It is not till lately that legiflators have thought of providing themfelves

---

* See Sect. 11, 21, 24, 26, 30, 47, 52.

with

with these necessary documents. They may be Sect. LX.
compared to the bills of mortality published an- p. 38.
nually in London ; indicating the moral health of
the community, (but a little more accurately, it
is to be hoped) as these latter do the physical.

It would tend still farther to forward the good
purposes of this measure, if the returns, as soon
as filed, were to be made public by being printed
in the gazette, and in the local news-papers.
They might also be collected once a year, and
published all together in a book *.

Section LXI. provides a penalty for es- Sect.
capes. This penalty, if the convict had LXI.
been ordered to hard labour in lieu of capi- p. 39.
tal punishment, is death : if in lieu of trans- Penalties
portation, in the first instance, an addition of on the
three years to his term of servitude ; in the party.
second instance, death.

---

* A few years ago, I began sketching out a plan for a
collection of documents of this kind, to be published by
authority under the name of *bills of delinquency*, with
analogy to the *bills of mortality* above spoken of : but the
despair of seeing any thing of that sort carried into execution soon occasioned me to abandon it. My idea
was to extend it to all persons convicted on criminal pro-
secutions. Indeed, if the result of all law proceedings
in general were digested into tables it might furnish
useful matter for a variety of political speculations.

O B.

OBSERVATIONS.

I cannot help entertaining some doubts of the expediency of capital punishment in case of escapes. *Punishments that a man has occasion to choose out of, should be commensurable.* That which is meant to appear the greater should either be altogether of the same kind, or include one that is of the same kind with the lesser; otherwise, the danger always is, considering the variety of men's circumstances and tempers, lest the punishment which appears the greater to the legislator and the judge, as being in general the greater, should appear the lesser to the delinquent. On the other hand, you may be sure of making your punishment appear the greater to the delinquent, when keeping to the same species, you can either encrease it in degree, or add a punishment of another species. A fine may to one man be worse than imprisonment; imprisonment may to another man be worse than a fine: but a fine of twenty pounds must to every man be worse than a fine of ten pounds; imprisonment for six months than imprisonment for three: so also must imprisonment, though it were but for a day, added to a fine of ten pounds, than a fine of ten pounds by itself.

In the present instance, it may very well happen, that a convict may even prefer certain death to his situation in a labour-house or on board a lighter: in such case, the punishment of death, it is plain, can have no hold on him. What is still more likely to happen is, that although he

would

would not prefer *certain* death to such a situation, he would yet prefer such a *chance* of death as he appears likely to be liable to, after having effected his escape. I say, after *having* effected it : for the *attempt*, I observe, is not made punishable in this manner.

It may be objected in the first case, that if death were preferable in his eyes to servitude, he would inflict it on himself. But the inference is not just. He may be restrained by the dread of future punishment; or by that timidity which, though it might suffer him to put himself in the way of dying at a somewhat distant and uncertain period by the hand of another, would not suffer him, when the time came, to employ his own. In either of these cases, capital punishment, so far from acting as a preventative, may operate as an inducement.

In cases of escape, little, it should seem, is to be done in the way of restraint, by means that apply only to the mind; physical obstacles are the only ones to be depended on. To the catalogue of these, large additions and improvements have been made, and still more, as I have ventured to suggest, might be made, if necessary, by the present bill. The degree of security which these promise to afford, seems to be quite sufficient without having recourse to capital punishment. This will save the unpopularity of inflicting a punishment so harsh, for an offence so natural.

In preference to capital punishment, I would

H 3   rather

Sect. XLI. p. 39.

rather be for applying hard labour for life. Such a punishment is already admitted of by this bill *.

Sect. LXII. p. 40. —on his affistants.

Section LXII. inflicts penalties on such persons as may be instrumental to escapes.

1. Any persons rescuing such a convict, either from the place of his confinement, or from the custody of any who are conveying him to it, or assisting in such rescue, are to suffer as for rescuing a felon, after judgment, from a gaoler.

2. Any persons, who by supplying arms, or instruments of disguise, or otherwise assist a convict in escaping, or attempting to escape, are to suffer as for felony.

3. Persons who, having the custody of such a convict, or being employed by one that has, permit him to escape, if *voluntarily*, are also to suffer as for felony.

4. If *negligently*, are to be deemed guilty of a misdemeanor, and are to be liable to a fine not exceeding ten pounds, or to imprisonment for not more than six months, or to both.

OBSERVATIONS.

The punishment here appointed for negligently permitting an escape, is, I fear, liable to be too

---

* See Sect. 52.

small;

fmall; efpecially confidering, that a wilful per-
miffion of this fort, may frequently, for want of
direct proof, be no otherwife punifhable than as
an act of negligence. If a convict of this ftamp
be a man of fubftance, as may fometimes happen,
he may be very well able to give an under-keeper
fuch a reward for his connivance as may very well
indemnify him againft the chance of lofing ten
pounds, and fuffering even a fix months imprifonment. What is remarkable, this punifhment is no greater than that which, in another
part of this bill *, is appointed for the trivial offence of fupplying a convict with prohibited meat
or drink. Inftead, therefore, of faying that it
fhould not be *mere* than the *quantum* fpecified, I
would rather fay, that it fhould not be *lefs*. At
any rate, it fhould contain fome imprifonment;
for, againft imprifonment a man cannot be fo
completely indemnified as againft fine.

I fee no punifhment for the *attempt* to refcue, or the affifting in fuch attempt: yet the
attempt to refcue is an offence as much more
atrocious than the affifting in a quiet attempt to
efcape, as robbery is than fimple theft.

What is the ufe of defcribing the punifhment
of a refcuer in a round-about way by reference?
why not make it felony at once? The ftanding
punifhment for the refcuing of a felon (meaning
a fimple felon) is no more than fimple felony.
It ought, however, to be greater, or elfe the af-

---

* Sect. 41, 55.

fiftin

fifting in a quiet attempt to efcape, ought to be
lefs: *otherwife the offender has nothing to determine
his choice in favour of an offence lefs mifchievous,
in preference to an offence more mifchievous.*

I take for granted it could never have been
the intention that, under this claufe, the refcuer
of a capital felon pardoned on condition, fhould
fuffer capitally.

Sect.
LXIII.
p. 40.
*Profecu-
tions* for
efcapes
facilitat-
ed.

Section LXIII. is calculated to facilitate
the profecution of perfons concerned in efcapes.

1. Convicts efcaping may be *tried* in the
county in which they are retaken.

2. In a profecution for an efcape or refcue,
or attempt to efcape or refcue, either againft
the convict himfelf, or any perfon aiding
him, the certificate above-mentioned (after
proof made that the culprit is the fame that
was delivered with fuch certificate) is to be
deemed conclufive evidence of his being the
perfon who was ordered to the confinement
therein mentioned.

OBSERVATIONS.

To fhew the beneficial effects of thefe provifions, in faving ufelefs trouble, the way would be
to ftate and explain the feveral rules of law which
they difpenfe with ; but this is a piece of infor-
mation that would not be very interefting to readers at large, and lawyers have no need of it.

Section

Section LXIV. appoints the mode of procedure for the recovery of the pecuniary
penalties inflicted by this Bill, when no particular method is prescribed *. It is to be
summary, before two Justices of the Peace:
the imprisonment, in case of failure, is to be
for not less than one month, nor more than
six. The other provisions are what are usually inserted in cases of summary procedure.

Section LXV. is another provision of
procedure dispensing, for the purposes of this
Act, with the general rule of law, that
Judges must be *in* the jurisdiction *for* which
they are doing business. It sometimes happens that the Court-house for a town that
is a county of itself, is the Court-house for
the county at large, but the Judges lodgings are not situate in both. It therefore
declares, that for the above purposes, they
shall be " construed and taken to be situate
" in *both*."

OBSERVATIONS.

Here the hand of the lawyer is visible; a
plain man would have contented himself with

Sect. LXIV. p. 41. Penalties to be pro- ceeded for *summari- ly.*

Sect. LXV. p. 41. Judges may do business *out* of their ju- risdic- tion.

---

* See Sect. 40, 55. See also Sect. 18, 41, 62, where
other modes of procedure seem to be intended.

saying,

Sect.
LXV.
P. 41.

saying, that a judge of the defcription in queftion might do fuch bufinefs as might be done at his lodgings, for any county, although he were in an adjacent one. But there never was yet a lawyer, who, when either would equally well ferve the turn, did not prefer a falfe account to the true one. The old maxim which, to another man would feem inflexible, " nothing can be in two " places at once," bows down before him. Thefe paradoxes are a kind of profeffional wit; which is altogether innocent in the intention, though not altogether harmlefs in its effects. This is no reflection on the author: it is only attributing to him, in common with every body, what no body is afhamed of.

Sect.
LXVI.
p. 41.
Claufes of
indemnity.

Section LXVI. allows perfons profe-cuted for any thing done in purfuance of this Bill, to plead the *General Iffue*; if the fuit terminates in their favour, gives them treble cofts: if againft them, and by verdict, exempts them from cofts, unlefs the Judge certify his approbation of the verdict.

Sect.
LXVII.
p. 42.
Limita-
tion of
actions.

Section LXVII. limits the place and time of fuch a profecution. The jurifdiction is to be that wherein the act was done: the time within fix months of it.

Sect.
LXVIII.
p. 42.
Prefent
act re-
pealed.

Section LXVIII. and laft, repeals the prefent Act, except with regard to fuch of-fenders whofe terms are unexpired.

O B-

OBSERVATIONS.

Perhaps the fimpler and more commodious way would be to take a fection by itfelf for giving the requifite continuance to the above terms, and doing what elfe is neceffary (for I fufpect that more may be neceffary) to prevent the unintended confequences of fuch a repeal ; and then in another fection, to repeal the act fimply and abfolutely.

Some hundred years hence, when concifenefs fhall be deemed preferable to prolixity, and the parliamentary ftile fhall have been divefted of all thofe peculiarities which diftinguifh it, to its difadvantage, from that of common converfation, the formulary for that purpofe may be as follows :

The act 16 *George* III. c. 43. *ftands repealed.*

The act 16 George III. may be repealed : but the memory of the propofer of it will SURVIVE.

SUPPLE-

SUPPLEMENTAL HINTS
AND OBSERVATIONS.

THE following obfervations, though they connect with the fubject of fection 1. could not well have been introduced previoufly to fections 30, 43, and 52.

Further advantages of hard-labour over tranfportation: 1ft, in point of divifibility.

Befides thofe ftated under fection 1. a farther advantage, which the punifhment propofed to be eftablifhed in the Labour-houfes has over Tranf-portation, is that of fuperior *divifibility*; by which means the quantity of it is capable of being proportioned with greater nicety to the different degrees of malignity in different offences. The punifhment of Hard-labour is divifible in point of *intenfity* as well as of *duration*; and a divifion of it in the former of thefe ways, is actually directed to be made in fection 43. That of Tranfportation is divifible no otherwife than in point of duration. In this point it is, in its own nature, indeed, incapable of being divided to as great a degree of nicety as Hard-labour is. Very little advantage, however, of this property of it has been made in practice. I am not certain whether there may not have been a few inftances in which convicts have been tranfported for as fhort a time as three years; but in general, the only terms in ufe have

8   been

been for feven years, for fourteen years, and for life. In the duration of the confinement in the Hard-labour houfes, as many different periods are allowed on one occafion or another, as may be marked out between one year and feven years. I cannot fee, however, why even a greater latitude than this fhould not be admitted of, efpecially on the fide of diminution; in other words, why a fhorter time than a year fhould in no cafe be allowed. One fhould think, that for many of the offences that are punifhable by tranfportation, a lefs term than one year, and for petty larceny, a lefs term than two years (the terms refpectively allowed of) might fuffice. But on this head I fhall infift no farther, as it would lead me from the particular object of the propofed Bill, to difcuffions that belong to a general furvey of criminal jurifprudence.

Another point in which the punifhment propofed by the Bill, has the advantage of Tranfportation, is that of being in the way of being *remitted* at any time on the ground of merits difplayed fubfequently to the offence. Provifion, we may remember, is made for that purpofe in fection 52. But a convict who is tranfported, though he be not out of the *reach* of pardon, is out of all *hope* of pardon on that ground, fince he lies out of the reach of all obfervation which could dictate the expediency of fuch indulgence.

—2dly, Of remifibility.

The following hints connect, in fome meafure, with the fubject of fection 13. and with a principle adopted in fection 40.

A fuitable

Motto and device for labourhoufes.

A fuitable *motto* over the doors of thefe houfes might have many good effects. It might contribute to inculcate the juftice, to augment the terror, and to fpread the notoriety of this plan of punifhment.

The following fentence might, perhaps, anfwer the purpofe :

Had they been induftrious when free, they need not have drudged here like flaves.

Or this,

> *Violence and knavery*
> *Are the roads to flavery.*

The latter is that which I fhould prefer on many accounts. It is more expreffive ; indicating more particularly the kind of mifbehaviour that was the caufe of their punifhment ; and the proverbial turn of it, together with the jingle, will render it more apt to be circulated and remembered by the people. *Violence* refpects thofe who may be committed upon a pardon for robbery, or thofe who may have been committed in any way for malicious mifchief ; *knavery*, the common run of thieves and fharpers. *Fraudulent* and *forcible*, is a divifion that runs in a manner through the whole catalogue of offences againft the police.

The efficacy of this motto might be ftill farther affifted by a *device*. Over the door there might likewife be a bas-relief, or a painting, exhibiting a wolf and a fox yoked together to

a heavy

a heavy cart, and a driver whipping them. The wolf as an emblem of violence and mifchief; the fox of knavery. In the back ground might be a troop of wolves ravaging a flock of fheep, and a fox watching a hen-rooft.

Bas-reliefs, if made in artificial ftone, might be caft, a number of them in the fame mold, and be the fame for all the Labour-houfes.

Should it be thought an improvement, a monkey, as being more peculiarly the emblem of wanton mif-chief, might be added to the above train. Among the offences which it is propofed fhould be punifh-able in this manner, are many that come under the denomination of malicious mifchief. In this cafe, the infcription, inftead of " *Violence and knavery,*" had need to be, " *mifchief, rapine, knavery.*" The danger is, left the addition of an animal, whofe manners are calculated more conftantly to excite merriment by their drollery, than difplea-fure by their mifchieveoufnefs, fhould give fuch a caft of ridicule to the whole contrivance, as fhould counteract the defign of it.

The device adopted in the houfe of correction at Mentz, and other foreign prifons, according to the account given of it by Mr. Howard *, does not feem fo well imagined as it might be. It confifts of a waggon drawn by two ftags, two lions, and two wild boars ; and the purport of the infcription is, that " if wild beafts can be tamed

---

* P. 108.

" to

" to the yoke, we ſhould not deſpair of reclaim-
irregular men." The equipage here repreſented,
has nothing in it that is very characteriſtic of the
perſons whoſe conditions it is meant to alle-
gorize; and there ſeems to be ſomething awkward
in making the hopes of ſucceeding, with regard to
men, reſt, as it were, upon no better footing than
the ſucceſs of the contrivance there imagined reſpecting brutes. I have read of hogs being now
and then employed in ſome parts of France to
help draw a plough. We have read of gods
and goddeſſes, and now and then, perhaps, a Ro-
man general in his triumph, who have been
drawn by lions; but I never heard yet of a ſtag's
being yoked to a waggon, either as a truth or in
the way of fable; much leſs appearance is there
of its being acknowledged for a known truth that
waggons may be made to draw with a team compoſed of ſtags, and boars, and lions.

Let me not be accuſed of trifling: thoſe who
know mankind, know to what a degree the imagination of the multitude is liable to be influenced
by circumſtances as trivial as theſe.

Site of
the la-
bour-
houſes.

With regard to the ſite of the building *, might
it not be a proper direction to give, that care
ſhould be taken to have ſuch a quantity of
ground all around the building included in the
purchaſe, as might prevent any houſes from being

---

* See Sect. 11.

built

built within such a number of yards distance ?
An establishment of this sort might, in some way
or other, afford inducements to people of the lower classes to settle near it. But the near vicinity
of any house might be productive of several bad
effects : it might facilitate escapes ; it would take
away from the sequestered appearance of the scene ;
it would put the convicts and their neighbours into
the way of engaging in conversations which might
be of prejudice to both.

With regard to such convicts as it may be
thought expedient to put to works of the sedentary
kind, it might be of use, on the score of oeconomy,
if such of them as have a trade of their own that
can be carried on in the house should be permitted to work at that trade in preference to another. Hatters, stocking-weavers, taylors, shoe-
makers, and many other handicrafts, might carry
on their trades in such a situation, nearly as well
as any where else ; so it were in the wholesale
way, and not for particular employers. The
trades that will be set up in the house for the
instruction of the convicts will hardly be of the
most lucrative kind ; and if they were, it can hardly
be expected that a man should earn as much at a
trade that is new to him, as at one he has been
bred up to. The difference would be so much
loss to the public during the time a convict continues in the Labour-house. But it might, besides
that, be a loss to him, and through him to the
public, for the remainder of his life : if his confinement has been long, he may have lost, by the

time

time it is over, a great part of his fkill. In the compafs of a few years, a courfe of Hard-labour may have irrecoverably deprived a man of that pliancy of mufcle and nicety of touch, that is neceffary in fome trades.

The convicts who come within the view of this inftitution, may be diftinguifhed into two claffes : the one confifting of malefactors by pro-feffion, who poffefs no honeft talent ; the other of perfons of different trades and employments, who have fubjected themfelves to the cenfure of the laws by an occafional deviation from integrity. The firft cannot but be benefited by the inftitution in point of talent, as well as in other refpects ; the others, howfoever benefited in other refpects, may, in many cafes, be fufferers in point of talent, if their induftry be forced out of its old channels.

F   I   N   I   S.

www.ingramcontent.com/pod-product-compliance
Lightning Source LLC
Chambersburg PA
CBHW030607270326
41927CB00007B/1078